# Survivor

*a true story of one mans war*

written and published by

## ROY E. HILL

Ex-Flight Lieutenant RAF VR

# FOREWORD

## by

## Air Vice-Marshall H. Gill, CB, OBE, RAF (Ret'd)

This is a splendid story – a detailed snapshot of a slice of life for an 18-year-old wartime recruit to the Royal Air Force. It gives an account of the initial processing procedure by which thousands of late teenagers, as volunteers for RAF aircrew duties, were subjected to the rigours of basic Service disciplines and an awakening of a very special brand of comradeship which still prevails.

The author goes on to describe his elation on being attested and assigned to an operational Lancaster Squadron (No.207) and provides an intimate profile of each of the six other members of the crew. The risks and dangers of Lancaster night operations are graphically exposed – so is the evacuation from their burning and terminally crippled aircraft on a dark night in the depth of winter 1944. (The debt owed to Irvin parachutes, to the young WAAF ladies who packed them and to Squadron Commanders who insisted on regular 'baling out' drill, is inestimable).

The period spent as a prisoner-of-war, with all its privations, is well documented – not least for its revelations as to the callous maladministration of the German P.O.W. Camp Stalag Luft 1.

And so to a particularly unusual and successful post-war aftermath by way of a pervasive latter-day search for former colleagues leading to on-site reunions and remembrances.

Altogether well written, extremely interesting and once started, very difficult to put aside.

# A DEDICATION

They say that everyone has a book in them. If that be so
– then this is mine.

I have to thank two ladies for aiding, abetting and
encouraging me in my efforts to resurrect the past,
before the memory becomes too blurred.

They are my wife Gill, for her unfailing optimism,
and Aunty Kathleen, who shared the last ten years of
her life with us here at Woodpecker, leaving behind a
legacy of love that still fortifies.

As I write this, poor old Woodpecker has taken a
battering from Mother Nature (for the umpteenth time
in its chequered history). The River Trent has invaded
us; there was eighteen inches of sludgy water
throughout the ground floor and we are having to 'camp
out' in our bedroom, pending lengthy renovations
downstairs.

But, in keeping with this books title – we shall
survive!

ROY E. HILL
Woodpecker Cottage
Girton
November 2000

# PREFACE

On 2nd April, 1988 I was 65.

This monumental milestone, which I had for so long been approaching with ever-increasing speed, was suddenly upon me – I was now officially a Senior Citizen. I remember rolling the phrase around in my mind; it had a sort of senatorial ring about it, so different from 'Old Age Pensioner', a title which could have been designed to mist the eyes, harden the arteries and stiffen the joints.

Fortunately, passing the demarcation line of 65 was not quite the traumatic occasion for me that it is for so many, as I had already enjoyed nearly seven years of 'doing my own thing'. I had taken an early retirement, in order that my wife Gill and I could start to realise a long cherished dream. Like countless other suburban dwellers, we longed for a cottage in the country, with room to breathe and where the tempo of life would be more leisurely. After years of searching and several near misses (property auctions are the ultimate in mental torture), we at last succeeded in finding and acquiring what we sought. It was a rather dejected looking semi-derelict Georgian farm cottage set in about two acres and was, as the estate agent succinctly put it, 'ripe for restoration'.

So the intervening years have been hectic, in the nicest possible way. Stage by stage, the property, which includes a barn and an array of out-buildings, has been transformed. The original cottage dates back to about 1730 and obtaining necessary building materials to enable us to retain as much of the aura of timelessness that enshrouds the old place like a cloak, has been one of the most exciting tasks. In addition, we have tackled and eventually subdued the large kitchen garden. Gill is an horticulturist and has taken great pleasure in creating a lovely garden from a wilderness, even to utilising mountains of weeds, which, when grassed over, give the garden added interest. Another innovation was to channel all rain-water from the cottage roof direct into two ponds, from which excess water eventually finds its way into a soakaway, on top of which a bog garden now flourishes.

For some years before we 'went rustic', we had been engaged in the breeding and showing of that most glamorous of dog breeds (or at least in our eyes), the Golden Retriever. The integrity and unswerving loyalty of these beautiful creatures sometimes makes me despair of the human race, which appears to be hell bent on self-destruction.

Since we left suburbia, our canine family has increased from four to ten and there's every sign that it won't stop at that. Gill is the acknowledged doggie expert and is deeply involved in showing (which admittedly fails to raise my blood pressure), judging and breeding. I enjoy being involved in the dogs' welfare – they are all personal friends and have as great a diversity of personality as we humans. Certainly I find that exercising them is very good therapy for my super-annuated body. So I suppose that, technically speaking, my occupation could be described as 'geriatric kennel lad, part-time!'

# CONTENTS

Walney Island, Winter 1942
Was I ever this young?

# CHAPTER ONE

# THE EARLY DAYS

On the occasion of my 65th birthday, my wife Gill had arranged for a surprise visit to Coningsby in Lincolnshire, where the Battle of Britain Memorial Flight, consisting of several Spitfires and Hurricanes and the sole airworthy Lancaster (at least in this country) is based and lovingly cossetted by a team of enthusiastic young airmen. I was thrilled at the prospect of a close-up look at these august veterans, especially the Lanc. The last time I had been in close proximity to one of this illustrious breed was on the night of 4th December, 1944, when, with unbelievable luck, I somehow managed to bail out of a blazing aircraft as it went into its death dive.

We were a small party for the visit, comprising Gill, our younger daughter Jennifer, son Robin, my brother Maurice and his wife and Aunty Kathleen, Gill's elderly aunt, who, although without children from her own marriage, was the acknowledged family matriarch. In the huge, echoing hangar our guide showed us firstly the various marks of Spitfires and Hurricanes included in the Flight. Somehow they seemed so small to be the bearers of such illustrious, historic names. My first impression of the Lanc was similar to when we were initially introduced, at Syerston aerodrome, just outside Newark, in the spring of 1944; a feeling almost of awe and reverence. It had and has, to me at any rate, a most remarkable aura, that perhaps in humans we would call charisma, a knack peculiar to itself, of combining lethal intent with a certain grace and elegance; in fact, a thoroughbred.

At first I couldn't put my finger on the difference between the City of Lincoln, as this flying survivor is so aptly named and those I had been involved with during W.W.II. Then I suddenly realised that she was SHINY! Her coat shone like the Brylcreemed heads of most of we youngsters who once so proudly flew this Queen of the Skies into the battleground that was Europe. I asked our guide about this glamour coat that she was wearing. It appears that the gloss affords extra protection against the ravages of time, in addition to which, he assured me, it gave the aircraft an extra ten knots.

As we strolled around her, my mind was a jumble with all the inevitable associations she recalled, of faces once so familiar, full of the exuberance of youth, only to be snuffed out like candles, to remain forever young in the memories of those fortunate to have survived. No good trying to permutate the whys and wherefores of survival and non-survival, because like war itself, it defies all the laws of reason and logic.

So, this momentous visit came to an end, with me striving to appear unmoved by it all and, I suspect, failing miserably. This old aeroplane, linked so inextricably with those heady days, set off a train of thought in my mind of all the ramifications and twists of fate that culminated in that last, desperate leap into the war-torn skies of Europe those many moons ago. Suddenly, it all seemed like yesterday.

I was born and raised in Fleet, Hampshire, which before the War, although officially labelled a town, was little more than a village. That, of course, was before the commuter boom, which in the early 50s took dozy old Fleet by the scruff of the neck and transformed it into an almost unrecognisable seething, bustling, typical London commuter town. Whenever I go back there (which these days is very seldom, as the Hill clan, once so numerous there, is now represented by a solitary maiden cousin) I have great difficulty in relating to the place, with the obliteration of so many once familiar land-marks and faces.

Fleet, tucked away in the north-east corner of Hampshire, forms a triangle with Farnborough and Aldershot, so we youngsters who grew up within its confines were subjected to influences from the British Army and Royal Air Force, their looming presence seemed to affect our thinking processes and indeed our life style. Almost to a man (or rather boy) when war came, we opted for the RAF, volunteering at a very early age, lest we become enmeshed in the khaki military machine, that, viewed from such close proximity, held no charm for us.

Farnborough is considered by many to be the cradle of British aviation. I remember vividly my Dad regaling me with hair-raising accounts of when Colonel Samuel Franklin Cody used to fly his box-kites from Laffans Plain which is adjacent to the aerodrome, when the 20th Century was, like Dad, but a pup. He was also an eyewitness when the redoubtable colonel met his untimely end, in August 1913.

So it was not surprising, in those halcyon days of my youth, when aviation was still a thing of romance and adventure, that I should gravitate at every opportunity to the perimeter fence at Farnborough, there to glean whatever information I could about all that was latest and best in British aeronautical design. I was not the only addict; there were four of us, all of a mind, intoxicated with the world of flying and all its aspects. It was the era of such legendary figures as Amy Johnson, Jim Mollison, Kingsford-Smith, Jean Batten and a host of others, whose fabulous achievements rang around the world and set our young pulses racing.

Whenever possible, we would high-tail it to Farnborough armed with sketch-pads, pencils and occasionally a box brownie, to list all the aircraft types with which we were familiar, and sketch or photograph any strangers. Many prototypes were put through their paces there. When an unknown flying machine made its appearance, we would move heaven and earth in an endeavour to identify it, even to the extent of holding de-briefing in one another's homes, comparing notes and sketches. For every type of aeroplane that was accepted for production, many fell by the wayside. Years later, when I was on the staff of No.1 School of Photography at Farnborough, I had access to a wonderful library of historical aircraft photographs and negatives (many of the latter magnificent glass examples), encompassing all the weird and wonderful contraptions that either took off or attempted to take off from that hallowed airfield. I was thrilled to be able to put names to several types that had eluded us in the 30s.

This practice of clandestine information gathering continued until after the outbreak of war, at which time security became much tighter. Nevertheless, on looking through a pile of old photographs recently, I came across a picture taken shortly before I joined up in 1941. It depicts a large, twin-engined aircraft in drab camouflage paint and there is a roll of barbed wire in the foreground. I remember vividly pointing my box brownie at this unknown monster. With my heart working overtime and my trigger finger twitching, I snapped and ran. Having developed and printed the film in an outhouse at home, the resulting picture was duly tendered for analysis, when one of our number pronounced it to be an Avro Manchester. This was before it made its début with Bomber Command, so it was quite a scoop. When, shortly after, the Manchester was subjected to its ordeal by fire, it was found wanting; its huge Rolls Royce Vulture engines proving to be unreliable. However, from it was developed the doyen of all W.W.II bombers, the immortal Lancaster. Co-incidentally, the first unit to be equipped with the Manchester was 207 Squadron, 5 Group, who sustained terrible losses. But more of that elite outfit later.

So when war was declared, our quartet of potential fighter-pilots and Air Marshals was ready, waiting in the wings, foolishly wishing the time away, longing for our 18th birthdays to arrive. It wasn't as much the thought of coming to grips with the Hun that attracted us, as becoming part of what was for us the *only* one of the fighting services worthy of mention – the Royal Air Force.

We had weaned ourselves on all the available literature pertaining to the fighter pilots of the original war to end all wars – W.W.I. Our heroes were such legendary figures as Albert Ball, McCudden, Mannock, Bishop, Guynemer, Boelcke and, of course, the Red Baron himself.

In the event, the Aircrew Selection Board, when confronted with our undoubted talent, totally failed to detect the underlying genius lurking just below the surface. Misguidedly we, who in the aftermath of the Battle of Britain were ready and willing to take over the mantle of the great, were destined to become respectively, a Navigator, who was to be killed on his first op., a Bomb Aimer, who also failed to survive, a Flight Mechanic, who after the War transferred to the RCAF, and a WOp/AG (Wireless Operator/Air Gunner). The three of us who were accepted for Air Crew duties were all eventually commissioned. I like to think that the Aircraft Recognition engendered by our frequent trips to Farnborough had something to do with that.

Initially, my own disappointment at not being selected for pilot training was acute. Perhaps the Selection Board figured that, as I had once helped my dad assemble a DIY wireless set and I was the owner of an air-gun, I was peculiarly suited to train as a WOp/AG. It so happened that I was among the last to be trained in this dual role. The powers that be decided it was unnecessary for one man to be proficient in both capacities when operating four engined aircraft. I would humbly question their decision, particularly when I recall a certain daylight raid over Holland, when our mid-upper gunner received a large chunk of shrapnel in the shoulder and I was able not only to replace him, but feel confident in so doing. It was, in fact, the only occasion I was able to actually vent my spleen on the Third Reich, to my intense satisfaction. However, I overrun my story.

A few interminable months after my 18th birthday, in 1941, I received the all-important communication summoning me to report to RAF Padgate. This name was familiar to untold thousands of aspiring young men, the cream of British youth, gathered together from every conceivable walk of life and section of society, all facing this new hurdle in life in their own individual way. Their one common denominator was the burning desire to come to grips with the evil monster that was devouring Europe and enslaving her peoples. The sooner this despot was brought to book and they could return to the comfort of their various homes and life-styles, the better. Had we known then of the terrible price to be exacted before the Nazi regime was finally overthrown! Thank God we aren't clairvoyant.

While not exactly a hayseed, I'd had a country-type upbringing and was rather overawed by my new life-style. However, uniforms (and service hair-cuts!) are great levellers. By the time we had all been through the sausage machine, the magical transformation had been achieved and I felt a little more able to cope.

Padgate was actually just a kitting out station, into which the hotch-potch of recruits entered, clad in a startling variety of clothes, with hair of varying length and style, to emerge after a couple of days like peas in a pod, cogs in a huge machine.

So it was that after this short, traumatic initiation into service life I found myself as one of a party destined to taste the delights of Blackpool. I had heard so much about Lancashire's tinsel town, but I'm afraid that reality was a bit of an anti-climax, rather like the Lord Mayors show without the gilded coach. Yes, Blackpool, like the rest of Britain, was in mourning. Even the Golden Mile along the sea front was as black as your hat; it was as if the whole place was in hibernation.

I was allocated a civilian billet at 44 Palatine Road, where the misses Lightbown were kindness itself, looking after me with almost maternal care. I had the dubious pleasure of sharing an attic bedroom with a swarthy character, who claimed to have played swing fiddle in Oscar Rabin's band. He would insist on scraping away on his violin for hours on end. Never have I heard *Begin the Beguine* and *Jealousy* so frequently and flagrantly mutilated. Somehow, that instrument has never since appealed to me.

Our time at Blackpool was spent square bashing, a necessary evil, getting and keeping fit and being introduced to the Morse Code. Lessons in the latter were conducted at premises situated above Burtons the tailors. It is said that from there, the term 'Going for a Burton', the widely used RAF slang phrase, originated. This could well be, as any cadet unable to transmit and receive at the required speed, was summarily dismissed from the course – it was instant death. Consequently, Morse tests were real cliff-hangers and I often wonder how many chaps are walking this earth today because of their inability to pass the Morse Code test at Burtons! A thought which gives rather a twist to the accepted meaning of 'Going for a Burton', with all its sombre connotations.

So it was with great relief that the Morse barrier was surmounted and I could live to fight another day. Blackpool in the dark, in the winter, on an Airman's pittance was just the antithesis of what I had expected. It was to be 30 years before I once again clapped eyes on Lancashire's Pride, this time in all its garish beauty. What a contrast! It was impossible to equate that glittering, throbbing fun-town, seething with humanity with the blacked out shell I knew in the oh-so-bleak winter of 1941.

My next port of call was No.2 Radio School at Madley, near Hereford, affectionately known as Madley-in-the-mud, for reasons all too apparent during those winter months – you couldn't move for the stuff! Up to and including this course, both Air and Ground trainee Wireless Operators trained together. Everyone, it seemed, had been innoculated with Morse Code fever. In our spare time, weather permitting, we would visit the nearby River Wye and from opposing banks relay messages to one another, using shaving mirrors to imitate the heliograph. It was great fun and instructional. The equipment we learned to operate was of the heavyweight variety used to contact aircraft from the ground. Wireless Ops., or 'Sparks' as they were called, had a universal reputation of being a bit 'wacky' and by and large, I think it was justified. It had a lot to do with endless hours spent chasing elusive signals through the ether, plagued by the ever present static, using rather rudimentary equipment. Somehow it all got to you and I'm sure was responsible for the somewhat zany popular image.

Soon, as a result of lots of PT and games, I was fitter physically than I had been since a schoolboy. Also, inevitably, we began to acquire service jargon. The RAF had quite a vocabulary all of its own, as we 'sprogs' (raw recruits) soon discovered. We were, of course, "erks", the lowest form of animal life and we longed for the culmination of the course, when successful cadets would be awarded their 'Sparks', a very distinctive badge, carrying, to our minds, great prestige and more importantly, extra pay. It would be the first step up the ladder. To fail would be a fate worse than death, the ignominy of re-taking the course, or being expelled to the nether regions, where erks, we were told, were made to perform unutterably menial tasks under the ghastliest of conditions.

In the event, no such crisis arose. When the results were posted, I found I had indeed surmounted the first hurdle in the race that was to take me, hopefully, to what I then considered to be the pinnacle of human achievement – to fly on Ops against Hitler's European Fortress.

# CHAPTER TWO

# MORSE MANIA

Following a well-earned fortnight's leave in the spring of 1942, I received orders to report to RAF Wing, which is near Leighton Buzzard in Buckinghamshire. I was posted as a trainee Wireless Op and received an introduction to the Wellington, or as it was colloquially known, the Wimpey. Little did I know what a profound effect this legendary aeroplane was to have on my life and survival only a few short months hence.

At Wing was No.26 OTU (Operational Training Unit) where newly formed crews became acquainted with each other and learned to work as a team. So much could depend on the crew spirit engendered during the months of intensive training. It was no secret that the losses sustained by the operational squadrons of Bomber Command were prodigious and although actual figures were, for obvious reasons, never publicised, rumours were rife and, if only half of them were true, we should soon lose the War through sheer lack of man-power!

Most of the Wimpeys were ex-operational aircraft, many of which didn't take kindly to the diet of 'circuits and bumps' they were called upon to digest. Despite the heroic efforts of the ground staff, who seemed to work non-stop night and day, the accident ratio was high and many an aspiring aviator bit the dust at OTU, without ever reaching the operational starting gate.

I found it fascinating to actually be in contact with the crews when they were airborne. I used to try and visualise the chap to whom I was 'talking' in Morse and was amazed at the diversity and style displayed in transmitting. It was just as great a variation as one finds in hand-writing. After a while, it was often as easy to identify a particular aeroplane by the 'trade-mark' of its WOp as by its call sign.

So my six-month stay at Wing came to an end. It had been a fascinating experience and an insight into the more serious aspects of service life. For the first time I became aware of the unique way that RAF personnel handled themselves when confronted with personal tragedy; the veneer of flippancy which they effected to hide private grief. I remember vividly trying to console a fellow WOp (a Waaf) whose boyfriend had been killed in a flying accident. She was actually 'talking' to him in Morse when the mid-air collision occurred and it was as though he had been killed while they were conversing.

So the mental toughening up process began on my 19-year-old mind. This, I was to discover, was even more important on an operational bomber squadron than any amount of physical fitness.

Just when I began to think the powers that be had forgotten my existence, I received my marching orders. It was to be Madley once again, this time for the Air Operations course.

Nothing much had changed at Madley, except that the mud was even more invasive. I was hoping to see at least a few familiar faces, but initially, no such luck.

Having been allocated a bed in a Nissen hut, I despondently surveyed my fellow internees. Where on earth were all my former mates? Surely at least some of them should have been recalled at the same time as myself.

Sitting on the next bed was a rather dejected looking figure, so obviously in the same boat as myself that I felt encouraged to break the ice and introduce myself. When addressed, he looked up and I beheld a face etched, as it were, in apathy. It was long and sallow, with the nose prominent and beak-like and a chin that receded almost unnoticed into the neck. Dark, lank hair hung over his forehead in Hitleresque manner, whilst on the upper lip a few straggling hairs strove for survival. The only redeeming features were the eyes, which were large, dark and lustrous and when I spoke, these focused upon me with a curious intensity. All in all, a more unlikely candidate for Air-Crew duties would be hard to imagine. When he spoke, however, it was in a voice of surprising depth and resonance, that entirely belied his looks.

We soon struck up an acquaintance, I can't call it friendship; he wasn't the sort of chap you could get to know that well, being reserved and shy. His name, it transpired, was Joe and behind that curious façade lurked, I suspected, a mind both active and alert.

This was quickly borne out when we started the course in earnest. He could absorb the theoretical stuff like a sponge, but when it came to practical application he seemed to be all at sea. As this more or less describes myself, only in reverse, it was mutually decided to pool our joint talents and help one another over the rough spots. It certainly did help, at least as far as I was concerned. He had a wonderful knack of translating text-book jargon into something that even I could understand; but I'm afraid that from his point of view things were a bit different. Try as we may, we just couldn't make his hands, which had the long, tapering fingers of an artist, obey the dictates of his brain.

It was about that time that I began to notice his absentmindedness. Occasionally, be it in classroom, Naafi, or even aircraft, he would drift into a world of his own, far removed from mundane things. Needless to say, this wasn't exactly an asset in the wartime RAF.

The flying classrooms at Madley were De Havilland Dominies and Percival Proctors and as all the flying was done over the mountainous countryside of North and Mid Wales and at comparatively low altitudes, there were only two kinds of flight: bumpy and bumpier. It was at the termination of one such flight, in a Proctor, that Joe first brought the searchlight of publicity (or should I say notoriety) upon himself.

In order to transmit, it was necessary to reel out a trailing aerial, by means of a ratchet wheel. This aerial was weighted with several sizeable spheres of lead, to keep it clear of the fuselage. The winding in and out of this potentially lethal weapon was duly recorded in a log-book.

I was never quite sure how it happened, but the simple fact is that Joe omitted to reel in. That in itself is no great crime, many an aerial has been lost in this way, finishing up entwined around some tree or farmyard gate, inconveniencing no one but the animals. On this occasion, however, a solitary figure was cycling around the perimeter track. It had to be, inevitably I suppose, the squadron CO! Joe's weighted aerial came scything through the air, hitting the bike with an almighty thwack, dumping both it and its illustrious burden into the quagmire of Madley mud alongside the track. I would have given much to have heard the remarks of that gesticulating figure. He was a man renowned for his command of the English language in all its aspects, but this situation must surely have taxed even his repertoire to the limit!

The story of Joe's 'super clanger' reverberated around the station and I felt certain it would be a case of good-bye Joe, but no. After an interview that he afterwards described as "just a bit dodgy", we were all amazed to see him back in the class-room. His inscrutable face gave nothing away and his replies to the barrage of questions that assailed him were masterpieces of evasion. He managed to complete the course without further complications, finishing high and dry at the top in the theoretical subjects and scraping through by the skin of his teeth in the practical.

As for myself, it was with great surprise when, on completion of the course and before any results were announced, I was summoned to appear before a commissioning board. Commissioned Officers in the wireless world were something of a rarity, and it was with some trepidation that I was ushered before this daunting array of brass-hattery, among whom I instantly recognised Joe's erstwhile victim. The subsequent interview is a blur; I remember desperately trying to slow down my vocal delivery, as I had always had problems in that direction, thought production always seeming to be one jump ahead of the speech mechanism. This sometimes produced rather strange oral results, a sort of vocal overdrive that tended to worsen in times of stress.

Shortly after this harrowing interview, the course results were announced and sure enough I had fared better than I had anticipated, thanks in no small means to Joe's fortitude and patience, which at times I must have tried to the limit.

After Madley, successful candidates were to be sent on an Air Gunnery course. The two previous intakes had gone to Canada and South Africa respectively, so speculation and rumours as to our own destination were rife. It is hard to describe the feeling of anti-climax when we read on the notice board that we were being sent to Walney Island, which may have a rather romantic sounding name, but in fact adjoins Barrow-in-Furness, with a wonderful view of Vicker's Armstrong's Shipyards! So much for my dream of sun-drenched beaches in far-away places.

# CHAPTER THREE

# BAPTISM OF FIRE

**M**y arrival at Walney was so very different from the last one at Madley, in that all cadets who had qualified as Air Operators reported to the new station on the same day. Joe and I automatically took up where we left off, as hut-mates.

His approach to firearms, of which he had no previous experience, was one of extreme timidity. When handling them he was forcing himself to do something that was completely alien to his nature.

At Walney, we flew in Avro Ansons and Boulton Paul Defiants. The former, affectionately known as 'Annies', were just about as reliable an aeroplane as the RAF ever put into the sky, but the latter was an entirely different kettle of fish. Having enjoyed a very brief hour of glory during the Battle of Britain and a rather longer period as a night-fighter, the Defiant had now been relegated to the training role and was universally feared both by its pilots and trainee gunners. Its landing speed, due to high wing loading, was too fast for most, while the undercarriage was a singularly temperamental affair which occasionally wouldn't retract, sometimes wouldn't drop and now and again would change its mind in mid-stream, retracting or dropping one leg only.

It was customary, when flying in Ansons, for four cadets to fire from the midships turret in turn, the target usually being a drogue towed by a Harvard. In order that the number of hits scored by each individual could be counted, the bullet tips were dipped in non-drying paint of four different colours, so that each hole in the drogue would have an identifying ring of paint around it. This may appear a little crude, but in practice was quite efficient.

It was our first trip and Joe and I were two of a quartet. I remember my colour was red and his blue. Having duly pulverised (we hoped) the target, we landed and waited impatiently for the Harvard to drop its drogue, so that we could count our score. On examination, I noted with some satisfaction a number of red-ringed holes, but Joe peered in vain for any sign of success. As we stood there, commiserating with him (he was the only non-scorer), two chaps in flying kit came puffing up, very red in the face. They were the Pilot and Winch Operator of the Harvard. After babbling away in a very un-RAF-like manner, they managed to convey to us the information that there were bullet holes in their rudder! Shaken, we hurried across to their aircraft to examine the evidence and there it was; a neat little row of perforations, running from left to right (come to think of it, it could have been right to left!) across the fin and rudder, in a line that, had it been extended, would have cut clean into the crew compartment! Need I add that the paint around the holes was

– blue! Poor Joe. He just stood there crestfallen; there was nothing that could be said when confronted with this damning evidence. I think he was wondering, as I was, just how far short the bullets had stopped. One glance at the perspiring Harvard crew confirmed that their thoughts were running along similar lines.

This being an obvious case for a Court of Inquiry, we refrained from quizzing the abject Joe, the whole business being so indefensible. He was removed from the course forthwith, pending the Inquiry.

I found the Gunnery Course most absorbing. Our main weapon was the Browning .303, which was standard throughout the service. We worked and worked at it until we knew it inside out and could strip and re-assemble it blindfolded. Although with its relatively small calibre (as opposed to the .5 used by the USAAF) it was regarded by many as some sort of peashooter. I was to discover a little later on, that in the right hands it could indeed be a most deadly and effective weapon.

On completion of the course, we were duly awarded our Sergeants stripes and Air Gunners brevets, both fantastic morale boosters and were fully-fledged WOp/AG's. They bundled us home on leave post-haste, lest we desecrate the flesh-pots of Barrow-in-Furness with our carousing.

I went still unaware as to my next port of call. Joe's inquiry was still pending and I was unable to see him, or trace his whereabouts.

At home on leave once more. It was grand seeing the family and old friends, but where were the rest of the quartet that had sallied forth in search of fame and fortune? Somehow our leaves never seemed to coincide. I waited impatiently for the expected missive to arrive in the post and at long last it came. I was to report to a place with the unlikely name of Halfpenny Green, near Stourbridge in Worcestershire.

As I approached the airfield, I was encouraged to see the familiar silhouette of my old friend the Anson crouching at dispersal. It transpired that I was to undergo further training in Air Operating and it was a school for navigation. In those days the Ansons undercarriage had to be wound up and down manually and after a few weeks of this, my forearms started to develop quite dramatically.

My stay at Halfpenny Green proved to be longer than anticipated. After about a month I was summoned to the CO's office, to be told that my commission had come through. I was to collect a kitting out allowance, pop into Weatheralls the outfitters in Wolverhampton, pick up a raincoat and 'cheese-cutter' hat, change the rank on my battledress to Pilot Officer and report to the Officer's Mess – just like that! Not at all the invitation into the exalted realms that I had visualised. Perhaps I had seen too many movies of passing out parades at Cranwell, or even the American Academy at West Point, with young fresh-faced cadets marching proudly past to the strains of a Sousa march, while their relations stood emoting in the background.

So, sparsely equipped and feeling very much a stranger in a strange land, I nervously sidled into the hallowed precincts. Thank goodness there were one or two familiar faces to be seen; I remember in particular a Signals Officer of the penguin (non-flying) variety whose name was Jannaway. We, his pupils, had dubbed him 'Duff-Gen Jannaway', rather an unkind sobriquet, but he came heroically to my aid and I was pathetically grateful.

As course completion drew near, I was asked if I would stay on as a Flying Instructor, as there was a dearth of them. Reluctantly (I was itching to reach operational status), I agreed and so spent six months accumulating flying hours on Ansons. It really wasn't so bad, as the cadets did the undercarriage-winding bit and those venerable old kites inspired confidence. There are, of course, exceptions to every rule and I'm thinking in particular of one occasion when, in very bad visibility, we almost took the top off The Wrekin. This mini-mountain rises like a giant carbuncle out of the surrounding plain and was always a thorn in our flesh in bad weather. During the course of the War it claimed several lives. However, we survived; it was my first near miss and the only incriminating evidence we brought home was a few odd twigs in an engine nacelle!

After a few months, my feet were itching. I felt rather a sense of guilt, as instructional jobs such as mine were normally reserved for those who had already been through the fiery furnace of an operational tour. In the Mess, the talk amongst my beribboned fellow instructors was of far more exciting things than flying Ansons on cross-countrys.

Consequently, it was with considerable relief that I received orders to report to Silverstone, quite an unknown name then, just another of the many airfields that had erupted like a rash over the length and breadth of wartime Britain. Little did I realise that, whenever in the ensuing years, the name of Silverstone cropped up (which of course it has done with increasing frequency) my thoughts would go back to a certain incident, stamped indelibly on my young teenage mind.

Silverstone was the home of 17 OTU and it was there, on a freezing cold day early in February 1944, that at long last I became one of a team. There were Pilots, Navigators, Bomb-Aimers and Air Gunners, as well as Wireless Operators. Most were fresh from their various training courses, but there were a few who, like myself, had been instructors in their various capacities. These were mostly intrepid souls who had already survived one tour, which usually comprised 30 operations. It was remarkable that, having tasted life in a front-line squadron, they should find life in Training Command infinitely boring and so volunteer for a further stint of operational duty.

It was RAF policy to encourage the various categories of Air Crew to intermingle and by common consent sort themselves into crews. What brilliant strategy! So different from the American system where crews were assembled on a production line basis.

So it was when the process of sorting out was complete, I found myself, by mutual agreement, crewed up with five kindred spirits, all of whom, incidentally, were NCO's – rank didn't mean a thing, it was personalities that counted.

The pilot was an Aussie named George Wall. He was large, gregarious, good-looking and a cricket fanatic. He was engaged to a girl named Enid, back home in Perth and carried a pocketful of photographs of her, which he would produce at every opportunity. He, at the ripe old age of 21, was about a year older than me. I had no idea, of course, what he was like at flying aeroplanes!

Arthur Clark, or Artie as he was called, was the Navigator and also hailed from Australia. Dark-haired and stocky, he was 31, elderly by Air Crew standards. Back home in Sydney he had lectured at university and had had great difficulty in obtaining release to join the RAAF. As we got to know one another, we came to regard him as a sort of wise father-figure, someone to whom we youngsters could go with our many and varied problems. We always received a sympathetic hearing and sound advice.

Bill Wulff, the Bomb-Aimer, completed our trio from Down Under. He differed greatly from the other two, being brought up in sheep country, near Wagga Wagga. He was tall and lean, very sparing with words (a most unusual Aussie trait) and his laid-back mien was the perfect foil to the affable George. I never knew Bill to get into a flap, whatever the provocation and his very presence gave the crew that very desirable asset in our particular calling – stability.

Lastly, there were the two gunners. Bill Turner was a shortish, balding north-country Englishman. He was an ex-army regular, who had transferred to the RAF (to get out of all that walking!). Very much a closed book with regard to his life outside the Service, we never did get to know how old he was, but we put him down as somewhere in the middle thirties. He had an impish sense of humour and when in his cups would reel off every popular ditty of the day. Soon we were to discover that he had a rather curious idiosyncrasy; he would never take off without urinating under his turret. This was sometimes a bit of an embarrassment, as there were frequently Waafs around at dispersal and the rest of us would have to go in a huddle around him, rather like a rugby scrum, while he performed his ritual!

The other gunner was a fresh-faced Scots lad, 'Jock' Sweeney. (I never did get to know his proper Christian name). He was a very cheerful character and he and 'Winky' took to one another on sight. It was very important to any crew that there was a good rapport between the two gunners; lives could depend on it. At 19, Jock was a year my junior, in fact he made me feel positively mature.

Silverstone was a recently built wartime airfield and we were to fly the ubiquitous Wimpy, with which I had more than a nodding acquaintance during my sojourn at Wing. As there was no mid-upper turret, it was left to the two gunners to decide who would, when we converted to four-engine types, take up residence in the rear turret. As soon as flying commenced, it was mutually decided that Winky was to have that dubious distinction. Statistics were very much against the rear gunner, or 'tail-end charlie' as he was often called. His chances of survival were even slimmer than the rest of us.

So now we were a crew of six and it only remained for us to collect a Flight Engineer, which we were scheduled to do on arrival at HCU (Heavy Conversion Unit) for our team to be complete.

The Wellington presented us with a real challenge. They were perhaps the best known and at least by their crews, the best loved twin-engined bombers of W.W.II and their ability to 'take it' was legendary. Despite its reputation for ruggedness, it had an unenviable record when it came to ditching, as its fabric skin had a habit of ripping away from the metal framework of the fuselage when contacting water at speed. Nevertheless, we did our ditching drill assiduously, tongue in cheek. Later I was to come in contact with a few lucky ones who lived through the trauma of landing in a Wimpey on water, but they were rarities.

The radio call sign at Silverstone was a bit unusual and is one of the few that still come readily to mind. It was 5HS, which in Morse parlance is ..... .... ..., an awful lot of dots and not the easiest combination to transmit clearly. Some of the ground operators were complaining that they were confusing the call sign with an 'erase' signal, which was a series of dots, without the gaps in between. Apparently it was not unknown for aeroplanes from other stations to be mistaken for ours, but despite protestations, no-one succeeded in changing it.

At Wing, casualties through accidents were high. On the day of our arrival, I witnessed the horrifying sight of a Wimpey failing to unstick and ploughing into a haystack. All the crew were lost and in the resultant fire, a noble aircraft was reduced to virtually nothing in about two minutes.

On another occasion two aircraft collided during a night exercise over the North Sea and again there were no survivors and no wreckage was ever found.

So, inadvertently, we began to adopt that casual veneer so much in evidence on operational squadrons. To an outsider, the banter and flippant manner in which our late departed friends were discussed would appear callous in the extreme, but in reality, it was only a façade behind which we hid our true feelings from the world and one another.

When we arrived, the weather conditions were atrocious. In order to keep the flying programme going, runways covered with snow and ice had to be cleared. So all available aircrew were pressed into service, shoveling salt from the back of slow moving lorries. Up and down the runway they lumbered and when we were all near exhaustion, the job was completed. After a shower and a meal, it was back to the flying grindstone – nothing must impede the production of the aircrews which were the very life-blood of Bomber Command.

After one energetic session, I was instructed by the Adjutant to report to a particular Nissen Hut that had been allocated for the use of commissioned personnel, providing a modicum of semi-privacy and a little more leg-room than was the norm.

I knocked rather timidly at the door of my new abode and the door was opened by a tall, rather gangling individual wearing the light khaki uniform of the South African Air Force. He was a Flight Lieutenant Pilot, but what immediately took my attention was his face, which was, for the want of a better word, just plain ugly! I couldn't quite pin it down – all the usual facial features were present, but somehow they didn't seem to gel. The nose seemed a little too large, as was the mouth; the face was angular, with the chin rather pointed, while the ears, large and fleshy, stuck out almost at right-angles. The eyes, however, were warm and friendly and when my new room-mate, who introduced himself as Johnny Thompson, gave me a smile of welcome, his face became animated – I liked him!

The room provided accommodation for two in what was, by Nissen Hut standards, comparative comfort; there was even a separate small area with washing facilities. We two had very little time to become acquainted, as in about an hour we were both scheduled to attend briefing. A night exercise had been laid on and the entire course was to participate.

After a brief chat, my new-found friend went into our little ablutions area for a wash and brush up – and started to sing. I sat spellbound; he was singing a popular ditty of the day, in a voice like an angel – the purest tenor I had ever heard. It all seemed so incongruous, that such a gorgeous sound should emanate from such an unlikely source. On and on went the song – "I promise you, each time the postman rings, my heart will be inside the envelope he brings" – I didn't want it to stop.

I saw him in the briefing room with his crew, a league-of-nations affair, with a couple of Aussies and two English lads; they gave the impression of being a happy team. The exercise was to take us over the North Sea in the direction of Denmark and was to act as a diversionary raid in support of more potent action by Bomber Command. It was to be our longest night trip thus far, lasting between 4 and 5 hours.

From our point of view the flight was quite uneventful. It was a dark moonless night, the only slight hiccup occurring when we experienced a degree of icing up, which was quickly counteracted when we lost height.

However, on our return, it was soon evident that we were minus two of our number – and one of them was captained by my new South African friend! All avenues were explored to try and trace their wherabouts – we were all hoping that they had landed elsewhere, but when morning arrived with still no word, an air-sea rescue operation was mounted. Despite all their efforts, nothing was found of the two missing Wimpeys – they had disappeared into the void without trace. The concensus of opinion seemed to be that somewhere over the dark, cold watery wastes of the North Sea, the two aircraft must have collided. In any event, they were lost and ten aspiring young men, with all their dreams and hopes, had perished.

While Bomber Command casualties were horrendous, somehow to fall without even reaching the operational starting gate seemed even worse, so utterly pointless.

After a couple of days, all hope having gone, I sat dejectedly on my bed as the Adjutants men removed Johnnie's pitifully small number of effects and I realised with a jolt that we had been acquainted for a bare two hours! And yet his personality had made such an impression on me that I experienced a feeling of personal loss.

For the first time, my 20-year-old mind had to grapple with a situation that was to become far too prevalent in the ensuing months, when on an Operational Squadron I was going to have to adopt the seemingly callous veneer with which Air Crew strove to hide their private grief as comrades-in-arms came and went with alarming frequency.

I remembered, as the last vestiges of Johnnie's occupation were removed, that the title of the song he had sung so lyrically was *We mustn't say goodbye*. We'd scarcely said hello!

As a Grand Finale, the course was to end with our introduction to operational-type flying, a flight (known as a Nickel) that would take us over occupied France. The object of our visit was to be the bombardment of that city of romance, Paris, with an extremely lethal load – propaganda leaflets!

So on 24th March, following briefing, we emerged into the murky evening and clambered aboard our rather elderly flying machine, a Mark X Wimpey (HE911) that had many operational hours to its credit, in addition to the interminable diet of 'circuits and bumps' endured at the hands of we fledglings. At long last we were all set, after the seemingly endless months of training, to strike our first blow for freedom.

Soon our old Wellington was waddling, in its own inimitable way, towards take-off point. The relief was almost audible as, with engines at full bore and vibrating in every joint, the old girl finally unstuck and nosed her way up into the gloom.

Having formated into the usual gaggle, we edged our way inexorably southward, towards the great unknown.

Things went smoothly and in a remarkably short time I was writing "Crossed Enemy Coast" into my log book for the first time, albeit with a somewhat shaky hand.

After about ten minutes we had our first encounter with flak. This onslaught was comparatively 'friendly', being ill-directed, but was nevertheless near enough to set the blood racing.

As we neared the French capital, the cloud-banks below us were illuminated by the inquisitive groping fingers of searchlights, trying ineffectively to pierce the overcast and cone us. Things were deceptively quiet as we swung on to our bombing run, with the nerves of all on board strung up in anticipation of the expected barrage. However, nothing untoward happened and we managed to dump our load of 'Bumff' fairly and squarely onto the Pride of France; it was, after all, a fair sized target! Having disgorged, we wheeled away, feeling almost guilty at the lack of opposition. Was all this talk we heard of aerial mayhem so much pie-in-the-sky? Within seconds, however, the clouds, hitherto our greatest allies, deserted us and in a flash the searchlight beams locked onto us. There we sat, feeling suddenly and terribly alone, dazzled by a brilliance that momentarily deprived the mind of thought and the body of action. Then, before our inexperienced reflexes could react, the sky around us erupted with a series of terrific explosions and simultaneously from the depths of the aircraft came the nerve-shattering clang of metal tearing its way through metal. We had been told by some of the old hands that the time to duck was when you could *hear* the sound of the detonations above the engine noise. How right they were, we were nearly deafened!

Having apparently survived the initial onslaught, George galvanised into action and commenced to throw our ancient aeroplane all over the sky, trying frantically to elude those tormenting beams of light. After what seemed an eternity, we managed to tear ourselves free and flew into blessed darkness. At first, nothing seemed amiss, except that from somewhere in the dark recesses there came an icy draught, accompanied by the flap-flapping of ripped canvas. Knowing the Wimpey's reputation for toughness, we began to feel quite optimistic. This feeling was soon shattered, as the voice of Artie crackled over the intercom. "Sorry George, but my radar's packed up." On hearing this disconcerting news, I turned to my radio equipment – it was dead as the dodo! As far as we could tell, the compass seemed to be one of the few instruments aboard behaving in a rational manner, so hopefully all was not lost.

Setting a course that would, we fervently hoped, bring us to the English coast at the right place, which was the Eastbourne area, we plodded our chastened way northwards towards home.

After an age, Artie said confidently that according to his calculations, we were about to cross the English coast. No sooner had he uttered the words than the plane was rocked by an explosion of great violence – another eardrum breaker! Someone, far below, had it in for us and was shooting with murderous accuracy. For the second time we heard the thud and shriek of shrapnel scything its white-hot way around and into us.

This time George's reactions were lightning quick. He threw the old bus into a screaming dive, yelling as he did so, "Where the **** are we?" to which Artie, no doubt feeling his reputation as a Navigator dissolving around him retorted, "I'm **** if I know!" Consternation reigned. We seemed, however, to have foiled the grim reaper yet again; that awful barrage had stopped. Fantastically, after a roll call, it was discovered that no one had been hit, although we knew our old chariot had taken a pounding.

After hasty consultation, we reached the inescapable conclusion that we were utterly and completely lost, so our only possible ploy was to steer in what we hoped was a northerly direction, keeping our fingers crossed.

After about ten minutes on our new course, the voice of Bomb Aimer Bill suddenly erupted on the intercom – "By my calculations, George, we've got enough juice left to last for about a quarter of an hour, so get your finger out and find somewhere, anywhere to land."

I had been tinkering ineffectively with my radio and while both WT transmitter and receiver were defunct, I reckoned that it was worth trying to contact the ground by RT. So it was decided to try our luck and make the Mayday (emergency) call. Remorselessly the vital minutes ticked away, while we lost all the height we dared, with five pairs of eyes striving to penetrate the all-pervading gloom. George's voice kept up the continual pleading on the RT but the only reply was a load of static. Then, just when despair was clutching at our vitals, a voice piped up on the intercom, "Very light on the port quarter!" It was Winky, with his distinctive Yorkshire accent, trying desperately to sound matter-of-fact and failing miserably; he just couldn't stifle his elation.

Our relief was beyond imagining; someone, somewhere, had not only heard, but understood us. With a Red Indian war whoop, George spun her round like a top, whilst I hurriedly fired our Very pistol in reply, using the appropriate colours of the day and it worked, thank God, it worked! Almost directly below us runway lights, like friendly glow worms, peeped up at us through the murk, a picture of ethereal beauty. We held our breath as George, with engines spluttering and petrol gauges on zero, brought our battered, tattered old relic in to land with scarcely a bump. As we taxied along the runway, he turned his big, sweat-streaked face and grinning from ear to ear said, "Well mates, God only knows where we are, but who gives a damn?" Yes, at that moment in time, life was very, very sweet.

Reassurance wasn't long in coming, however, for as we slowed to a halt a crowd of wraithlike figures emerged out of the swirling mists, all jabbering away with such a nasal twang that Bill laconically remarked, "Strewth, but I reckon we've flown clear across the Atlantic!" Actually, we'd done nothing quite so spectacular; our port in a storm turned out to be the airfield at the Gloucestershire village of Down Ampney, occupied by the USAAF, who were operating Flying Fortresses (B-17s) from there.

The Yanks instantly made us welcome and gazed at our 'Rag Ship' (their nickname for the fabric covered Wellington) as though it had suddenly arrived from Mars. Come to think of it, we were more than a little curious ourselves, so we climbed down stiff-legged and took a stroll around her, making a mental note of the damage sustained. She really was a sight to behold; it was incredible that we had come through unscathed and that she had manoeuvred in so airworthy a manner after taking such a mauling. There were jagged holes you could put your head through in both wings and fuselage, with great naked areas where the fabric had been ripped away, revealing the aircraft's bones, resembling some huge, metallic honeycomb. It was no wonder our newly found friends gaped; to their eyes we must have looked like something the cat dragged in.

Having contacted Silverstone and arranged for a repair crew to fly down and patch up our old warhorse, we settled down, with no great reluctance, for what transpired to be a three day stay as guests of the American Air Force.

The day following our arrival was a Sunday. After an enormous breakfast (by British war-time standards) we retired to the anteroom and proceeded to carry out a sort of post-mortem on the extraordinary events of the previous night, which seemed to have no more substance than a nightmare. Had we really come through that holocaust without a scratch? One gaze out of the window was enough to confirm it. There she was, squatting on the tarmac for all the world like some huge, moth-eaten, prehistoric monster.

We were pleased to find a supply of English Sunday newspapers in the room and as I idly sat there perusing the *News of the World,* my eye was arrested by a small item tucked away in the stop press which ran: "Last night there was a hit-and-run air raid on Eastbourne at 10pm. Damage was negligible. The enemy force, a comparatively small one, was preceded by a lone raider." That was all. I read it through again, attracted perhaps by the word Eastbourne, so recently uppermost in our minds. Then, sitting as in a trance, realisation suddenly dawned upon me; it all fitted together like a jigsaw puzzle. Excitedly, I called to the rest of the crew and they came crowding around me. One glance and Artie, his eyes agleam with the light of battle, made a dive for the door, to re-emerge seconds later, brandishing his rolled maps and charts aloft like a sword. Spreading these out on the table, we scrutinised them carefully. Yes, there could be no doubts, it all dovetailed so neatly. According to his dead reckoning, we had been slap over the centre of Eastbourne at 10pm and he had in fact done a remarkably fine job; we'd been bang on course. It was just the long arm of coincidence (and our rotten luck) that we happened to be just one jump ahead of a Staffel of Ju88s, Eastbourne-bound! What, we wondered, were the odds of that happening on any trip, let alone your first?

At the end of three days, the repair crew had worked wonders on our old Wimpey and there she stood, looking, with her multitude of freshly doped patches, as though she was suffering from an acute bout of measles.

Nevertheless, she was pronounced airworthy enough to be flown back to Silverstone, so, with a certain amount of misgivings, we made ready to depart.

Our American buddies came out in force to see us off. They seemed sentimentally attached, not to us, but to the bedraggled apparition that had suddenly descended on them out of the void. They couldn't understand how an old 'Rag Ship' such as ours could take such a fearful buffeting and then in only three days be fit to take to the air again.

So, laden down with 'Camels' and 'Lucky Strikes' we climbed aboard, feeling considerably older than the last occasion we had done so. Was it really only three days?

Back at Silverstone, what to us had been a great hair-raising adventure, was duly recorded in terse service jargon, that reduced it to just another flight, quite commonplace in comparison to many, but to us it had been a real baptism of fire, etched forever on our young receptive minds. For us, no matter what the future held, this particular battle-scarred old Wimpey would always occupy a very special niche in our hearts. We considered ourselves to be members of what must be quite an exclusive band; those who had the dubious distinction of being shot at (and hit!) by both friend and foe on their first flight into enemy territory.

Our arrival back at Silverstone was very much an anti-climax. Most of the crews had already gone on leave. What on earth was the use of having a line to shoot if you didn't have an audience! Before we left for a well-earned rest, we were instructed, after our leave, to report to Winthorpe aerodrome, just outside Newark, in Nottinghamshire. Curiously, it is situated about six miles from where I now sit, struggling to recall the details of those momentous happenings of long ago.

CHAPTER FOUR

# STIRLING DAYS – ENTER THE LANC

Winthorpe, along with countless other airfields, was constructed during the early months of the War and was a satellite of pre-war built Swinderby, which was still going strong as an active airfield until recently.

Nowadays, what was then RAF Winthorpe, is now the Nottinghamshire County Show Ground, where all manner of public functions take place. Also, it houses the Newark Air Museum, where I sometimes have a nostalgic browse. It is quite a sobering thought that without exception, all the aircraft on display were in service *after* we did our stint there in 1944!

The only planes that fly from Winthorpe these days are gliders, or rather sailplanes and one or two light aircraft used for crop-spraying.

However, I overrun my story by about 45 years!

It was at 1661 HCU (Heavy Conversion Unit) Winthorpe we were introduced to four engined aircraft in the shape of the Short Stirling. It was a large, well constructed, but rather unwieldy machine. Although relatively well appointed by W.W.II bomber standards, it was unpopular with many of its crews (although some thought very highly of it), owing to its inability to fly as high or fast, with or without a full load, as the Lancasters and Halifaxes which comprised the remainder and majority of the four-engined bomber force. Consequently, when flying operationally, every endeavour was made to ensure that the timing of the bombing runs were sufficiently staggered. Nevertheless, it only took a small discrepancy to create havoc for the poor Stirling crews, who were almost as much at risk from being hit by bombs from above, as by flak or night fighters.

We had rather an unfortunate introduction to the Stirling, which was unusual in being an all electric aeroplane. (Most types used hydraulics for various functions). As we all know, electrics are fine until you blow a fuse!

Our new CO took us for a tour of the establishment and we couldn't help noticing an aircraft circling the aerodrome with one undercarriage leg dangling incongruously. This was much more noticeable on this type, as the Stirling's legs were no less than fourteen feet long; the resultant effect was rather like a one-legged stork in flight. In these circumstances, it was supposed to be possible to wind the undercarriage manually, but obviously this had been tried but to no avail. Apparently this particular bird had been in trouble for hours and was circling in order to lose petrol and so lessen the fire hazard on landing.

A couple of hours later, we stood entranced as the ungainly machine made its landing approach, with the crash tender and fire engines standing by at the ready. With great skill, the pilot touched down with his 'good' leg, which was the port one, on the extreme right hand side of the runway. Then she lost speed, tilting inevitably to starboard and as the wing dug into the soft earth, she swung and shuddered to a standstill; a wonderful feat of airmanship, resulting in a damaged wing, a couple of bent propellers and precious little else.

Before we commenced flying, we had to collect a Flight Engineer, the seventh crew member. He turned out to be another 19 year old sergeant, Eric Dunn by name, a handsome, wavy-haired lad who had been reared in Kent and Liverpool. Quiet and studious, he fitted immediately into the crew's international jig-saw. I think that he and I operated on the same introvert wavelength, which helped to counterbalance the extrovert antics of some of the others – I am thinking of George and Winky in particular. Eric, as befits an engineer, was very much of a mechanical bent and was never happier than when tinkering with or talking about engines, be they in motor-bikes or aeroplanes. Of all the crew, he had the closest rapport with the ground staff, who had my unbounded admiration. They worked ridiculously long hours, often under the most wretched conditions, in order to keep their particular warbird airworthy.

On several occasions, I took the Aussies home to Fleet, where they made a great impression on my family and friends. I remember while we were at Winthorpe, we had a 48 hour pass, so George and I decided to get home by hook or by crook. Hitchhiking was never my strong point, but with George it was so easy. He would stand by the roadside, select the vehicle of his choice, then saunter into the road and flag it down, just like a policeman.

This time we elected to try the A1, hopefully making our way to Fleet via London and George selected a real beaut. It was a Rolls Royce and it was not until he had risked being run over going through his 'policeman' routine that we noticed that the car sported a pennant! In the back was a real live Air Marshal, en route to the Air Ministry in London. Never before had we been in close proximity to such an exalted service personage. He really proved to be a most pleasant and affable travelling companion and on arrival in London, he shook hands and wished us luck. George, typically, put a hand on his shoulder and said, "Good on yu' mate, hope you're around next time we hitch." He never was.

Flying in the Stirling was, after the Wimpey, a relatively luxurious affair. The WOp even had a window with a view and a chair with sheets of armour plating underneath and at the back of it. No other plane that I know of was so equipped, the extra weight being deemed too great a price to pay. I must admit that it gave one a sense of security. One WOp I got to know quite well at a later date, who *almost* survived a tour on Stirlings, told me that whenever there was any flak flying around, he would swivel his chair round so that the armour plating was between him and it – makes sense to me.

After a few weeks of concentrated training, we had welded into quite an efficient team and were considered to be proficient in the handling of large aeroplanes. The nearest we came to action was when we were dispatched on a couple of diversionary raids, which involved approaching the enemy coast, but not crossing it. Both these trips went off without a hitch, in fact our ride at Winthorpe proved to be a very smooth one, after the trauma of Silverstone. Nevertheless, I think all our pulses accelerated a little when we learned that we were being sent just a few miles down the road to Syerston, where we were to be introduced to an aircraft that was already a legend in its own very short lifetime – the fabulous Lancaster. Syerston was a brick-built, pre-War station and seemed very orderly and civilised after the Nissen huts of Winthorpe and was the home of No.5 LFS (Lancaster Finishing School).

The 'Lanc', since its introduction the previous year, had amassed a tremendous reputation both within and outside the service and was lauded by Aircrews and Ground Staff alike, so naturally we were full of curiosity. First impressions can be deceptive, but in this instance, all the hearsay was not only upheld, but exceeded.

We were driven to dispersal for a closer look at this four engined bomber par excellence. Initially I had one or two misgivings, as we walked around then clambered into her. The obstacle course that masqueraded as a fuselage was to say the least a bit off-putting, it seemed almost to have been designed to obstruct movement. Compared to the Stirling it was very cramped and austere, although I noted with satisfaction that the WOps' quarters were adequate, if spartan and not too claustrophobic.

But it was when the engines were started up that the great transformation took place. The machine became instantly alive as we gazed along the wings from the 'drivers seat' and one by one the four engines were run up. As the volume of sound grew and the vibration made her pulse with life, we listened enthralled to the song of the Merlins, giving the impression of limitless, unbridled power, a sound unforgettable to all those who, throughout the War years, were connected with this wonder engine from Rolls Royce, which arguably did more to win the War than any other single factor.

Yes, we were all hooked and we couldn't wait to put this aeroplane through its paces in her natural element. I remember 'Butch' Harris describing the Lanc as the 'Shining Sword' of Bomber Command. I can think of no more apt description.

She certainly seemed to have some sort of extra dimension and after our first short flight we were all under her thrall. There were no apparent hidden vices and in the air seemed to behave with almost ladylike docility, which somehow didn't equate with her aggressive persona, clad as she was in camouflage paint, with guns bristling from her like porcupine quills.

We continued where we left off at Winthorpe, except that we were very much aware that this was 'it', that it was on this type that we were destined to reach the goal that we had all spent years striving for – flying on Ops.

Much time was spent on 'baling out' and 'ditching' drills. The latter wasn't so bad, but the former was purgatory for me. The WOp, when the order to abandon aircraft was given, had to leapfrog over the front and rear spars and past the mid-upper turret (and numerous other bits of impedimenta designed to impede) to the rear entrance, or rather exit, door, situated just in front of the tail. Not too arduous the first time, but, when repeated over and over again, wearing full flying kit, on a warm summer's day, it became something of an endurance test. However, the importance of these drills couldn't be overstressed, as it was vital that, should the emergency arise (and all the statistics made this a distinct probability), all seven of us would respond immediately, doing the right things without hampering one another.

We were very keen, as a crew, that everyone should have a smattering of each other's jobs – just in case. In a way, I was one jump ahead, being a fully fledged gunner. Navigation, about which I'd had some instruction, I found fascinating, especially when propounded by Artie; he really had the teachers knack of bringing his subject to life. Also, it was important that he and I collaborated in our jobs, especially when it came to taking astro-shots, at which we were both proficient and operating the various kinds of radar then in use. These, without getting technical, were used as navigational aids and to give early warning of impending attack. They rejoiced in such names as 'Gee': 'H2S': 'Fishpond': 'Aural Monica': and 'Visual Monica', to name but a few. I often wonder who was responsible for those unlikely and rather exotic names. Although these were the early days of radar, the rate of technical progress was phenomenal and Navigators and WOps were forever attending courses on the latest brainchild of the Boffins.

So the WOp's job grew in complexity, although his basic functions were keeping in touch with base and relaying wind speeds, which were broadcast at regular intervals, to the Navigator. (It really is amazing how much winds can vary in speed and direction at varying altitudes). Another aspect of the job was the obtaining of 'fixes' by means of D/F (Direction Finding) bearings. At various points throughout the UK beacons were transmitting signals, giving an identifying letter followed by a long, constant note. The WOp would obtain bearings from the two, or sometimes three beacons, by means of rotating a small, circular aerial set atop of the fuselage. These readings were then plotted on a chart and where the lines from the signals crossed was, hopefully, the present position of the aircraft. 'Fixes' thus obtained weren't necessarily very accurate, owing to the plane's speed and the fact that readings were not taken simultaneously. But very often, especially when other navigational aids were impaired, the old D/F played an invaluable and in many cases, a life-saving role. Lastly, radio contact was vital in an emergency; many a crew lived to fight another day because of prompt action by the WOp, transmitting vital information concerning an aircraft's position just prior to ditching, or forewarning base or anyone of a myriad of landing fields of damage sustained or crew injuries, so that emergency services would be available with the minimum loss of time.

But learning the basics of actually flying the Lanc was what gave us the biggest kick. We would all, under George's watchful eye, fly her straight and level, then graduate to gentle manoeuvres and a carefully monitored touch-down. The feeling of having this huge, noisy leviathan under control was really quite a heady experience, but we all hoped fervently that we would never be called upon to employ our newly-found skills.

As for the Bomb Aiming and Flight Engineering functions, I never really got to grips with either of them. Anyway, I figured it most unlikely that I should ever be called upon to operate a bombsight and I never could master the mysteries of a motor-bike engine, so didn't consider much of my chances when it came to getting to grips with Rolls Royce Merlins.

As the course progressed, with its quota of Circuits and Bumps, cross-countrys, bombing practices and fighter affiliation exercises, we really became conversant with our new mount and despite the rumours about horrendous casualties that leaked through the grapevine from the front line squadrons, our confidence grew day by day. We were determined that, whatever the future held, we, by honing our skills to the maximum, were going to give ourselves the optimum chance of survival. As for lady luck, we all knew how great a part she played in the proceedings and there was no legislating against her.

As the end of our stay at Syerston drew nearer, we were scheduled to fly on yet another diversionary raid. On several occasions we were briefed, but fickle weather resulted in a succession of stand-downs. After one such postponement, we all adjourned to the camp cinema, which was an elongated Nissen hut. Vividly I recall sitting entranced as Judy Garland, one of my favourites, cavorted about the screen. The film was *Strike Up The Band* and to my dismay, about halfway through, the projector was stopped, the lights went on and the order was given for all aircrews to report to their aircraft. So off we went, straight from the fantasia of Hollywood into the darkened skies of war-torn England. Curiously, to this day, I have never seen the remainder of *Strike Up The Band!* Perhaps, one day, when they are showing golden oldies on TV, I shall.

These days when I travel along the A46 towards Nottingham, which I do frequently, as I pass a semi-derelict but still recognisable Syerston aerodrome, I glance to the left and there, set back from the road, among the trees is a very disreputable Nissen hut, stacked full with bales of hay and a varied collection of farm machinery. Yes, it is the old camp cinema; I chuckle to myself and whistle a few bars of *Strike Up The Band*. Then I have to pay particular attention to my driving, as I have a habit of rolling back the curtain of years and walk again with those irrepressible young blades, so many of whom were so tragically cut off in the fullness of their exuberant youth.

Soon the day of reckoning arrived and we were given our marching orders. We were to report, after a short leave, to Spilsby in Lincolnshire, deep in the heart of 5 Group country. We'd heard lots about the '5th Air Force', which it was sometimes known as and how it often operated alone. One snag with flying the super-efficient Lancaster, which could carry more bombs at a greater speed and for greater distances than other types was that, inevitably, I suppose, they got lumbered with the marathon trips, often being airborne for upwards of ten hours on some flights.

CHAPTER FIVE

# MY OPERATIONAL DEBUT

Two squadrons operated from Spilsby, which was a satellite of East Kirby; they were 44, a famous Rhodesian outfit and 207, which was to have the dubious privilege of adding George Wall and crew to its illustrious ranks.

It was now July 1944, not long after 'D' Day and the bomber countryside of Lincolnshire reverberated to the sound of aircraft engines, day and night.

I arrived at Spilsby alone. It was easy to find the RAF station; you just followed your ears! On approaching the airfield, it was my nose that began to twitch, there really was a most ghastly stench emanating from somewhere alarmingly near. My mind went to secret weapons and biological warfare, but it turned out to be my first encounter with a Billy Goat! Sighing with relief, I plodded onwards, eager to see what life was like on a real, live, operational squadron.

Spilsby was almost identical to countless other airfields constructed during the early War years. I've read somewhere that the mammoth task of converting England into a gigantic aircraft carrier was the single largest feat of construction ever achieved by man. Be that as it may, there is no doubt that in some instances aerodromes were rather too close to one another for comfort. I remember when we were at Winthorpe, there were some hair-raising incidents when aircraft in the circuit rubbed shoulders with those from Swinderby, just down the road. Things weren't that bad between Spilsby and East Kirby, but it was a hazard that had to be watched.

It was the policy of the RAAF (Royal Australian Air Force) in 1944 to commission all air-crew on becoming operational. So it gave me great satisfaction to be joined in the Officers Mess by George, Bill and Artie. For too long I had felt out on a limb, sometimes envying the NCOs their camaraderie, but now things had changed for the better, in fact, at one stroke, the commissioned members of the crew outnumbered the non-commissioned and selfishly I was elated.

In contrast to Syerston, we were once more 'relegated' to the more austere Nissen huts. As a consequence of the round-the-clock flying, there were people sleeping at all times day and night. The ear-battering caused by Lancs flying low and others being engine-tested was considerable, but such was the exhausting tempo of squadron life, that I never heard anyone complain of insomnia.

My three Aussie friends and I shared the same hut. We awoke early one afternoon, having been out all night on an exercise. George, who slept in the raw, had just got out of bed and was stretching luxuriously when suddenly the door opened and there, framed in the doorway, was the rather dumpy form of Cynthia, our roly-poly batwoman, clutching a tray of steaming mugs of tea! Her face registered a mixture of surprise, terror and delight and then, as though she was taking part in a Brian Rix farce, she screamed, dropped the tray and bolted. What a waste of tea! Afterwards, when the resulting hubbub had died down, she claimed she had knocked, but it must have been a very timid tap. For ages the poor girl blushed whenever our paths crossed. I think the shock of being confronted with 15 stones of naked Aussie masculinity was just a bit too much for her.

We soon settled down into our new mode of life. Casualties, as in all front line Bomber Command squadrons, were alarmingly heavy, with only a very small percentage of crews surviving the 30 Ops that comprised a tour. Consequently, there was a pretty constant influx of new faces and a corresponding exodus of the more familiar ones. Sometimes crews would arrive and disappear ghostlike into the void with bewildering suddenness. Strangely, one felt a sort of detachment from it all; it wasn't like trench warfare, where men witnessed the horror going on around them. Except when an aircraft limped home shot up, little was seen of the carnage that was exacted almost nightly over Europe. It was a strange cocooned war, when for the first time in history men would leave the relative comfort of home and comrades and sally forth into the unknown, to face whatever fate held in store for them.

The chances of surviving, in the event of being shot down, were minimal. It is frightening to think that Bomber Command lost more aircraft during the course of the War than there were men who survived, to either become POWs, or make their way home by courtesy of the French Underground organisation.

On one of our final training flights, I had rather an embarrassing experience. We had been airborne for a couple of hours and not only did I feel on top of my form, I felt positively exhilarated. The world was a wonderful place and I could do no wrong. Why then was the intercom full of babbling voices and why was Artie hovering around, behaving in such a strange way, all agitated and red in the face? Gradually, the feeling of omnipotence receded and I was normal enough to take in the information that I'd omitted to plug into the oxygen supply! Apparently, the rest of the lads had been amazed at the amount of utter drivel I had been broadcasting over the intercom and I looked aghast at my Log Book, which was full of a load of gibberish. Luckily, Artie had twigged the cause, recognising the symptoms of lack of oxygen and plugged me in. Thankfully, no real harm came of the incident, but when I thought about the possible implications, I broke into a cold sweat. We had, after all, been flying at over 20,000 feet. That, needless to say, was the first and last time I transgressed; it was a lesson learned the hard way.

One day, all flying having been cancelled because of fog, which is prevalent in that area near the east coast, I was propping up the bar in our local, The Bell, feeling a bit jaded after the oxygen debacle, when suddenly there emerged from the sea of faces around me a ghost from the past – Joe! I just gaped. I'd heard nothing of him since Walney and had assumed that his somewhat chequered career was over. But there he stood, twice as large as life, a fully fledged sergeant. I hesitated momentarily, debating my method of approach, then finally sidled up to him. He greeted me with a slow, hesitant, smile and after the beer had broken the ice a bit, we started to reminisce, carefully skirting around one or two odd incidents. I thought it best to let any explanation come from him, but when none seemed forthcoming, my curiosity got the better of me and I asked him point blank about the Walney incident. I might have saved myself the trouble; he merely muttered something inarticulate about getting into a muddle with the deflection, but I knew this wouldn't have stood up for a minute at a Court of Inquiry; after all, that drogue did happen to be about 300 feet astern of the Harvard! However, this being the sum total of all the information he was willing to volunteer, I let the matter drop – but this didn't stop me from wondering, indeed marvelling. It would have taken a Houdini to wriggle out of that one.

I saw quite a bit of Joe during the next few days. He and his crew had a few 'shake-down' flights prior to going on the real thing. Then the great day arrived, Joe and I were to be christened on our first Op. It turned out to be a daylight raid on Brest, to bomb some German battle-ships in the harbour there. How ironic, I thought, when nearly all our training had been channelled towards night-flying and our first taste of action was to be without the cover of darkness, which we looked upon as a sort of friendly blanket.

There had been several previous raids on Brest, all of them abortive; apparently the area was a hot-bed of flak. So optimistic we were not, it definitely wasn't an ideal target for an operational début.

After briefing, I sought out Joe, to wish him well, inwardly consoling myself with the thought that there wasn't much chance of his shooting down a Lanc, as WOps only went into a turret if one of the gunners was hit.

Then, laden with impedimenta, we clambered into the canvas covered truck and were whisked out to dispersal, feeling rather like moles above ground in our unaccustomed sunny environment.

We went through all the usual pre-flight checks like automatons, with the adrenaline working overtime. Take off went smoothly enough, on this, the first time we had left mother earth with a cargo of real, live bombs. She certainly seemed to take an unconscionable time unsticking, but after by far our longest take-off run to date, she managed to stagger aloft. One thing about daylight, at least you can see your compatriots and flying in close proximity to them was a good morale booster. From my astro-dome look out point, I had a grandstand view of this formidable armada as it droned on a south-westerly course. Up to this point, we had been like race-horses straining at the leash and now here we were about to tackle the first hurdle; with each man secretly wondering how he would react when it came to the crunch.

We crossed the South Coast and nosed our way out over the sea. Thus far, except for the bottled-up emotions, it had all the hallmarks of a training jaunt, but we were under no illusions. As we swung in from the Atlantic towards Brest, we saw in the distance a black, man made cloud. The guns were giving a warm reception to the first wave of Lancs and as we headed towards the target at what seemed a snail's pace, the whole scenario seemed unreal, due mainly to the amount of engine noise generated by our four labouring Merlins, which effectively blanketed the external bedlam. It was rather like watching one of the old silent movies, but in glorious technicolour. Once again I remembered the old adage about only worrying about flak when you could hear it; true enough, you couldn't hear this lot, but it didn't stop my stomach from tying itself in knots.

Relentlessly, we ploughed our way into the maelstrom, there was nothing to be done but sit still, like an aunt sally and hope for the best. This was where lady luck either smiled or frowned upon you. As we swung onto our bombing run, I was horrified to see a Lanc on our starboard beam suffer a direct hit and literally disappear in a blinding flash, followed by a shockwave which threw us perilously close to another aircraft to our port. Then all that remained was a funeral pyre of greasy black smoke, out of which emerged a solitary engine, propeller still rotating, cartwheeling grotesquely into the depths below. One second a machine, a monumental example of man's ingenuity (and arguably his stupidity) manned by seven aspiring young men, all with an unquenchable zest for life, with hopes and dreams far removed from the horrible blood bath into which they had been precipitated and then in the blinking of an eye, men and machine liquidated. In that instant of time, wives became widows, children became fatherless and families devastated, never to be the same again; and to think that all Air Crew were volunteers! There is something in human make-up that I shall never fully understand.

I dragged my eyes away from that awful spectacle and I became aware of the fact that Bill was intoning instructions to George on the intercom: "Left, left," "Steady," "Right". His voice was low pitched and steady as a rock, he almost sounded bored! Exactly the panacea my over-stretched nerves needed. Then suddenly it was: "Bombs away, let's get the hell out of here!" As he spoke, directly beneath my feet there was a sharp, metallic clang and thinking we had been hit, I automatically recoiled, my knees finishing up under my chin. Within seconds I realised, rather shamefacedly, that this phenomenon was caused by the bomb retaining gear rapping against the Lancs underbelly when the bombs were released. But why had nobody told me this would happen? I peered around the corner where Artie sat Buddha-like at his Navigator's table. He had seen my antics and was grinning like a Cheshire cat. He, it appears, had been forewarned.

With ill-concealed relief, we finally emerged from the black cloud that overhung the target like a pall and high-tailed it for home. Despite the intensity of flak, we had come through completely unscathed, at least physically, faring far better than many others.

That evening, we adjourned to The Bell and there, glass in hand and propping up the bar, was Joe. For once, his poker face was illuminated with a wide grin, which transformed his visage in quite a remarkable way. I enquired how things had gone with him and the grin widened still further, leading me to suspect that he was a little under the weather; but no, he assured me, this was his first pint. This was an entirely new Joe, obviously bubbling with an inner excitement. Operational flying, I knew, affected people in widely different ways, but his reaction was a complete enigma to me.

After a couple more drinks, he, for the first time in our acquaintance, wanted to talk, to unbottle this hilarious something that was convulsing him. The story came in fits and starts, punctuated by bursts of infectious laughter. In a voice about half an octave higher than its usual resonant bass, he said: "Well, Roy, things went pretty well at first and the sight of all those Lancs all around gave me a wonderful feeling of security, I might even say immunity. We saw nothing of either flak or fighters until we neared Brest, when we had to sit tight and plough through that bloody awful barrage; it put the fear of God up me, I can tell you. But apart from a bit of buffeting, we weren't touched. Then, just as we were about to start our bombing run I suddenly realised, in a moment of blind panic that the trailing aerial, which should never have been out in the first place, was dangling beneath the fuselage! When the bomb doors opened, they would foul it, with heaven knows what consequences. Like a shot I bent down to the ratchet wheel and was frantically winding when, just above my head, there was the most almighty crash and I remember thinking – Joe lad, this is it. For a bit I crouched there, the old heart thumping nineteen to the dozen, trying in a dazed way to make sense of the bubbling crescendo of voices coming over the intercom. Then, as nothing untoward seemed to happen, I gingerly raised myself up to a sitting position. A howling gale was blowing from somewhere, very near and then I saw them, two bloody great holes you could have kicked a football through, on either side of the fuselage, smack in line with my head! I realised that, but for my own stupidity in forgetting to wind in, I should, without the shadow of doubt, have been a headless hero. The irony of the situation gripped me and involuntarily I began to laugh and have been doing so ever since."

He paused to wipe his moist eyes and took a swig of beer. The bar was beginning to fill up and fearful lest other ears should get wind of the "clanger of my life," as he afterwards referred to it, he promptly retired into his shell and switched the conversation to other topics.

At his request I refrained from broadcasting the matter, as we two, he assured me, alone knew the whole truth. He must have had a heck of a job explaining to the rest of the crew, not to mention the groundstaff, how he came to be in the land of the living, considering the location and extent of the damage incurred by the Lanc, which curiously had received very little damage, apart from Joe's "bloody great holes". I've no doubt, however, that with his past record, the concoction of a suitable alibi would be well within the range of his capabilities.

There was great relief at surviving this initial journey into the unknown. No matter how much you tried to picture it and talked about it to the veterans who had been through the operational mill, it was impossible to visualise the traumatic mental build-up to the great occasion. Everyone reacted in his own individual way and it's all an unknown quantity until put to the test.

As for myself, I had thus far in my short life come to know the true meaning of the word fear on two occasions. Firstly, during the thrashing that had been administered to our beloved old Wimpey by 'us' and 'them' and secondly when, on the bombing run over Brest, when our Lanc seemed to be suspended timelessly in space and I desperately wanted to get out to give her a push!

There was no possible way of knowing what effect ever increasing doses of the same medicine would have. At the time I was rather haunted by the tragic story of a Warrant Officer Air Gunner. He had already completed one tour with distinction (he had been mentioned in despatches) and had volunteered for a second. Half way through it his nerve went and he found it impossible to continue. He was duly branded with the dreaded L.M.F. (lack of moral fibre), stripped of his rank and banished to the nether regions. The ludicrous fact is, of course, that if he hadn't, of his own free will, offered himself for further Ops, he would undoubtedly still be a WO, his character unbesmirched. I found it impossible to come to terms with this despicable practice.

Later I was to discover that a friend whom I knew at Madley (in fact, we two were the only ones to be commissioned from our course), suffered the same ignominy. A nicer chap you couldn't wish to meet. I admit that for the sake of morale, it is necessary to prevent anyone so afflicted from flying operationally, but to be cast on life's slag-heap (for that is what it virtually amounted to) was, I contend, inhumane and heartless.

In celebration of our début, the whole crew, along with many others, went in to taste the flesh-pots of our nearest sizeable town, Skegness, universally known as Skeggy. As a toper, I was not in the same league as some of my more seasoned colleagues, but was determined not to let the side down. I vaguely remember being in a pub, jam-packed with figures in Air Force blue and being jostled hither and thither. Sadly, that is all I can recollect, as the next thing I recall was waking up on my bed back at camp, laying there half-dressed with the mother and father of all hangovers. On my bedside table was a little silver cup which I'd never seen before. It was inscribed 'Beer Drinkers Challenge Cup, Winner'. Bemused, I turned my aching head and beheld George, Artie and Bill, looking paternally down upon me, grinning like a trio of benevolent gargoyles. In response to my questions they assured me that there had been a contest in the pub and the first one to drink a gallon was awarded the cup. To my certain knowledge, I knew that eight pints was way beyond my capacity, so who were they kidding? For the remainder of our stay at Spilsby, I had to endure the slings and arrows of my crew-mates, as well as most of the squadron and it was considerably later, under very different and unforeseen circumstances, that I was eventually to get to the truth of the matter.

CHAPTER SIX

# AERIAL MAYHEM

Our operational career, having taken its first stumbling step, seemed to take ages getting into its stride. The east coast is notorious for its fog and the mist that rolls in from the North Sea. We seemed to be plagued by stand-downs, which did nothing at all for the nerves. Sometimes we would even get to the stage of climbing aboard, all hyped up for take-off, when cancellation would be announced. Poor old Winky used to get into a terrible tangle with his ritual and would curse the powers that be for their hesitance, which he felt was directed at him personally.

Eventually, the flying programme began to gather momentum and we started to collect a few scalps. The majority of flights were still made during the hours of darkness and despite the fact that there was always a greater chance of collision then, we felt less vulnerable, particularly as our defensive armament was designed to be effective at short range.

When I use the word defensive, there was the odd exception to the rule. The CO when we arrived at Spilsby was a Wing Commander Grey. He and his crew were adept at using the Lancaster as an *offensive* weapon and many were the tales of daring that percolated through the squadron. One yarn had it that they used to stooge around over the Third Reich with their navigation lights on, challenging the night fighters to have a go. Be that as it may, at least some of the unlikely sounding stories must have been true, because at the end of their tour, they had no fewer than 8 notches on their guns – all confirmed night fighter kills! Win'co Grey's gunners were Wallace McIntosh in the rear turret and Larry Sutherland was mid-upper. This talented, highly decorated pair succeeded in shooting down three night-fighters within the space of 20 minutes on one trip. As far as I know, this feat was unique, a Bomber Command record. Very few fighter pilots could boast that sort of performance.

As for we lesser mortals, clashes with night-fighters were to be avoided like the plague whenever possible, although usually we had very little choice in the matter. For use in case of attack, 5 Group had developed its own cork-screw manoeuvre, a series of violent gyrations designed to induce air-sickness even in the toughest constitutions. Attacks were usually mounted and broken off at great speed, often before the gunners could bring their guns to bear. The majority of combats, where the bomber survived, were inconclusive, although many an Air Gunner hopefully claimed a 'possible', after a frenzied exchange of fire. So confirmed kills were rare and in the main fighter-bomber clashes were terribly one-sided affairs. One only has to refer to the enormous number of 'kills' claimed and substantiated, by many

German fighter pilots. They make the claims made by their allied counterparts appear trifling.

One of our early Ops was to the Baltic, to do a spot of 'gardening' (mine-laying) and turned out to be the nearest thing to a doddle possible. Everyone clamoured to do these trips as they counted as a full operation and let's face it, easy targets were hard to come by. We duly 'wave-hopped' over the North Sea, 'hedge-hopped' over Denmark, dropped our mines on their watery target and returned to base without a shot being fired in anger by either side. As George remarked at de-briefing: "Thirty of those would do us fine!"

Shortly after, another pending 'gardening' job was announced and it was to involve two Lancs from 207. Such was the demand, that it was decided to draw lots for the privilege of another 'piece of cake'. We cursed our luck at losing out on this one, but the following morning neither of the lottery winning crews had put in an appearance back at base. Later that day it was confirmed that both had been 'jumped' by night fighters over Denmark. As we had done, they were flying very low and as a result had no time to bale out. Lady Luck can be fickle at times!

At about that time, another drama unfolded. Four Halifaxes, or as they were usually referred to, 'Halibags', were diverted to Spilsby following a raid. It was one of the few occasions that visibility in our area was better than elsewhere. With an airman's curiosity we clambered all over them, weighing them mentally against our own chariots. Along with the Lanc, the redoubtable Halibag bore the brunt of Bomber Commands assaults against Europe during the War's later years and has never, to my mind, been held in public esteem to the degree its record deserves. They certainly gave the appearance of being tough, durable aeroplanes, perhaps lacking a little of the Lanc's elegance, but with a rugged solidarity all of its own, due perhaps in some degree to those great rectangular tail-fins.

The day following their arrival (1st November), with the Halifax crews no doubt sleeping off the effects of their exertions, 207 was scheduled for take off on a daylight raid to Hamburg and we were among those selected. As we trundled from dispersal and around the perimeter track towards take-off point, we looked across as the first heavily-laden Lanc lumbered forward, slowly gathering momentum. Then the unbelievable happened: as it accelerated, it started to swing to port and we watched aghast as it ploughed straight into the first of the Hali's, which were parked neatly in a line. We held our breath, waiting for the big bang (our bomb load consisted of a 4,000lb 'cookie' and masses of incendiaries) which, thank goodness, never materialised. The two aircraft entangled, immediately catching fire, which had a knock-on effect, setting light to the other three Halifaxes. The Lancaster crew, captained by PO Loveless, were on their first Op and were to be seen leaving their aircraft like corks out of a bottle, disappearing into the distance at a rate of knots.

The only casualty was a Halifax Flight Engineer, who had heroically tried to rescue his burning plane and was overtaken by the flames.

PO Loveless and crew were, surprisingly, to survive their tour, against all the odds, although I understand they wrote off two more Lancasters in the process!

Amazingly, after all the mayhem, the runway was almost clear and serviceable and although take-off was temporarily delayed while debris was cleared, we eventually got airborne in time to catch up with the remainder of the force. I subsequently learned that of the 20 Lancs scheduled to fly on the raid, only 13 of us managed to get airborne. The remainder were all unairworthy, suffering in varying degrees from flying metal.

Fortunately, there were no further casualties on that trip, but the atmosphere in the Mess that evening was one of shell-shock. What had indeed been a tragedy could have been carnage on the grand scale.

By the time we returned, the Halifax crews had departed for their base at Middleton St. George, no doubt thanking their lucky stars that they had not all been on board their ill-fated charges.

Although we didn't know it at the time, 1944 was the crunch year for 207, along with many other front-line squadrons. Over 400 air-crew were to perish, in addition to those already taken prisoner and many others wounded. But at the time, we weren't interested in statistics, only survival and the long climb towards the magic 30 mark was painfully slow. After completing the first ten, we were granted a fortnight's much needed leave and I was amazed on my return to Fleet, to find that everything was so *normal*. It gave our existence at Spilsby a nightmarish quality, as I started trying to enumerate all those intrepid souls who, during those last hectic weeks had vanished from my ken.

It was during this leave that I heard of the demise of one of our original quartet of hopefuls. Colin and I had many shared interests, in particular sports and athletics. His speciality had been long-distance running, for which his sparse, lean frame was ideally suited and I used to pound the streets, helping him with his road-work. Our service careers had run on somewhat parallel lines; he too had been commissioned, as a Bomb-Aimer and had flown in Wellingtons at OTU but whereas I had gone on to the four-engined types, he had been posted to the Middle East to serve in a Wellington squadron. At that time the Bomber Command strike force was almost completely comprised of the newer, larger types, but abroad the old Wimpey was still very much a front-line aircraft.

Colin was an inveterate gambler; always had been. He would bet on anything and everything, from horses and dogs to two flies crawling up a wall and he was invariably lucky. But his luck ran out when he and his crew disappeared on the day that the mainland of Italy was invaded from Sicily. No trace of man or machine was ever found. I visited his disconsolate mother, trying unsuccessfully to choose appropriate words for the occasion – there aren't any.

It is one thing to lose a relatively new acquaintance, but when that person is a lifelong friend, the grief felt is far greater and deeper. So I returned to Spilsby saddened by this personal loss, to face once more the future, in which I knew only too well that the odds of pulling through were stacked heavily against me.

However, I managed to throw off my feelings of foreboding when I met up again with the rest of the lads. They all seemed rejuvenated after the break; the three Aussies had visited Scotland and were full of talk of Lochs and haggis. We were airborne within hours on an HLB (High-Level Bombing) exercise, over the Wainfleet bombing range with a VIP aboard, the Station Commander. It appears there was a bombing competition within the Group, in which all OCs were invited (or instructed to participate) and our particular Group Captain had chosen George Wall and crew to carry him aloft and help him plant his practice bombs near the target. We did better than that; with Bill's connivance (was that cheating?) it was well and truly straddled and an elated Groupie declared his confidence in winning, which we took to be a feather in our caps.

The euphoria of this little status trip was soon dissipated when, on landing, we were just in time to be briefed for a night operation and the target was to be Harburg, just across the river from Hamburg. Suddenly, my recent leave seemed years away. We had joined 207 just after the Battle of Berlin, but apart from the German capital we were chalking up quite an imposing array of primary targets, which included Munich, Nuremburg and Essen, all places with formidable defences. When the wall map in the briefing room was uncovered to reveal any of these places as the target for tonight, you could feel the tension in the room. In those days non-smokers were rare (I smoked a pipe) and the atmosphere at briefing and de-briefing usually resembled one of those pre-war London pea-soupers.

Harburg, true to form, proved a formidable obstacle to surmount, with flak and fighters in abundance, but we seemed to lead a charmed life and despite the daunting casualty lists, our confidence was growing with each flight – we were going to be the exception to the rule and confound all those depressing statistics.

It was now October 1944 and the land-battles were raging in France and the Low Countries. We were briefed for a daylight raid on the Walcheren islands, just off the Dutch coast. The target was the sea-walls and the object was to flood the area and create chaos among the German troops still occupying the area. We felt quite confident about this one, as it was only a short trip which was virtually a hit and run attack, of the type I remember Jerry once carried out in Eastbourne!

We homed in towards our objective, with not a fighter in sight and only sporadic flak – this looked like another 'piece of cake'. Then, just as we dropped the bombs, jerry opened up with the heavy stuff, ruffling our composure. This time we *heard* the detonations and our Lanc started to buck in a most alarming fashion and behind me I heard the unmistakable whine of shrapnel. Suddenly, over the intercom came a cry of anguish, which ended abruptly. From my vantage point in the astro-dome I looked towards the rear; at first nothing seemed amiss and then I noticed a neat hole drilled into the perspex dome of the mid-upper turret and poor Jock slumped forward over his guns. Having relayed this information to George, I scrambled back down the fuselage and with Artie's help, managed to unbuckle the mercifully unconscious Jock from his harness and laid him out on the rest-bed. There was lots of blood and from a cursory examination it appeared that quite a chunk of metal had entered his right shoulder leaving a jagged wound. We did what we could, injecting morphia and applying dressings. It was vital to get him home as soon as possible; despite our efforts he was still losing blood. Leaving Artie to tend to Jock, I, for the first and last time on Ops, strapped myself into the mid-upper turret. There was a fearful draught whistling through the damaged perspex and never in my life have I felt so utterly isolated and exposed, with my head and shoulders high above the fuselage. We had, by this time, cleared the target area, but were still being dogged by flak and the plummeting silhouettes, which I recognised as FW190s were hurtling down upon our gaggle of plodding Lancasters. Winky, alert as ever in the rear-turret, yelled out: "Dive Starboard – Go!" simultaneously opening up with a long burst from his four brownings. As the fighter, his attack frustrated by our manoeuvre, did a climbing turn past us, I swung my guns and opened fire, watching the tracer curling towards him. Now I knew the meaning of blood lust; at last I was able to hit back with something more tangibly lethal than a morse key and the feeling of power was intoxicating. The Focke-Wulfe, showing no visible signs of damage, promptly disappeared into a cloud and we lost touch. I still like to think that we drove him away; maybe that's wishful thinking, but it was something to have survived a full-blooded onslaught against a fighter with all the advantages of speed and fire-power.

With the injured Jock aboard, George pulled out all the stops on the return journey. I vacated the turret and contacted base, alerting them of our situation. The ambulance ran alongside us as we touched down and whisked Jock away, still unconscious and ashen faced. We heard subsequently that, following a large blood transfusion, the removal of the shrapnel and a comprehensive stitching job, there was every hope of a full recovery, but it meant the breaking up of our team and introducing a replacement gunner.

At de-briefing we described our combat and Artie reckoned he had seen smoke belching from the Focke-Wulfe as it entered the cloud, but no-one else could confirm this, so we hadn't the temerity to claim a 'possible'.

Our new mid-upper turned out to be one of the 'elder statesmen' of Bomber Command, Ted Sharpe, a 39 year old Flight Sergeant who had accumulated quite a few Ops, but had lost two crews in doing so. We desperately hoped we wouldn't be the third! He was a quiet, almost introverted sort of chap, quite a contrast to the ebullient Jock and old enough to be his father.

As a result of damage sustained from flak, our usual Lanc was sent in for repair and the day following our eventful daylight trip over Holland, we learned that we were down for a night raid on Dusseldorf, slap in the middle of the industrial heart of the Ruhr, or Happy Valley as some Bomber Command wag had dubbed it. To make matters worse, we were to fly in an old reserve aircraft and one of my fellow WOps told me with a twinkle in his eye, that when this particular kite took off, the rear spar, which was just behind the radio compartment, moved appreciably under the strain – not a very comforting piece of information.

To say that we were apprehensive would be a masterpiece of understatement. Nevertheless, after praying for the stand-down which never came when most needed, we found ourselves climbing aboard this museum-piece, hoping against hope that the pre-flight checks would produce something, anything, to prevent us taking off, but no such luck. By take-off time all aboard were convinced that 'the sign' was upon us. Even George, never at a loss for words, seemed quiet and pensive and Winky went through his ritual without a ribald comment.

Sure enough, as the old girl strove to get airborne, I could feel the main spar moving, or I suppose undulating would more correctly describe it and the vibration was something that had to be experienced to be believed.

After leaving the English coast behind, George asked the gunners to test their

*Taken on last Leave,*
*November 1944*

guns. This was routine, to make sure that, should the necessity arise, we should be ready for instant action. Unbelievably, when Winky was testing his 'four of a kind' in the rear turret, his voice piped up: "Rear turret gunsight U.S." There was quite a list of eventualities that could cause a 'Boomerang', or return to Base. Most were of a mechanical nature, but some, like the failure of an illuminated gunsight, were electrical.

I'm sure that, had we been in our own Lanc, we should have pressed on regardless, but George clutched at the defect and after getting me to go back and corroborate that the gunsight fault really was bona fide and not repairable while we were airborne, he promptly jettisoned the bombs, about turned and high-tailed it back to Spilsby. The relief on board was something to savour and tongues that had been strangely silent started to wag with a vengeance.

In the case of a 'Boomerang', an event not at all uncommon, there was often an element of suspicion and questions would be asked. In our instance, the Gunnery Officer and armourers gathered around our rear turret like flies around a honeypot, but try as they may, they couldn't get Winky's gunsight functioning, so it had to be a workshop job. Later I button-holed our veteran rear-gunner and in answer to my questions he said: "I don't understand what all the fuss is about. The bloody thing didn't work, so we had to come home, didn't we?" But you should have seen the glint in his eye when he said it. To this day, I wonder – did Winky pull the wool over everyone's eyes? Be that as it may, we all drank his health in The Bell that night.

We had by now completed 17 Ops, over the half-way mark and way past the average crew's life expectancy, which at that time was about 11 trips; what a depressing statistic! It was strange to think that we were now one of the more senior crews. Ted Sharpe had settled into our scheme of things and was quite happy to be the butt of Winky's droll Yorkshire humour.

Eric, our engineer, was the only one of us that was mechanised, having returned from leave with his motorbike, which he tended with loving care. Occasionally he would take me for a ride through the flat Lincolnshire landscape and for the first time I began to realise life outside the camp continued in much the same way it had done for centuries. When the War was over and we interlopers were gone, the locals would still talk of the old days when Lincolnshire reverberated day and night to the cacophony of aero-engine music and of the thousands of young hopefuls who came and went like Will-o-the-wisps, leaving behind them the stuff of which legends are made.

CHAPTER SEVEN

# WE BITE THE DUST

I t was 4th December, 1944 and as we reported to the briefing room, all eyes, as usual, immediately focused onto the wall-map. The ribbon didn't stretch very far, just across France and into the Ruhr Valley to Heilbronn, and no-one seemed to have been there before. (I was to learn much later that this was the one and only time during the whole War that Heilbronn was visited in any strength by Bomber Command). The very mention of the infamous 'Happy Valley', probably the most heavily defended area in all Germany, was enough to set the nerves twitching. But at least this time we had a proper Lanc; we had taken delivery of a brand new one, PB765, or "B' Baker, as we called it.

During the seemingly endless five years of the War thus far, many an aircraft had fallen to the intense, awesome flak curtain thrown up by the Germans to protect their industrial heart, not to mention the hordes of night-fighters that seemed to be forever prowling there.

Our target was the railway marshalling yards. According to Met., visibility over Heilbronn should be adequate, but we were warned to expect low rain-clouds soon after turning onto our homeward leg. Consequently, we were briefed to fly low, just under the cloud-base, thereby making it hard for the night-fighters to get at our vulnerable underbellies.

The trip seemed to be progressing favourably enough and we managed to bomb the target, already well illuminated by the time of our arrival, with only moderate flak opposition, compared to some of the rousing receptions previously encountered.

Shortly after turning homewards, we ran, as expected, into heavy cloud. George, as per briefing, steadily lost height, trying to get below cloud-base, but it was nowhere in sight. Artie said we had to watch it, as we were approaching the Rhine valley and shortly after crossing the river we would be heading towards the Vosges mountains. So it was decided to abandon the flight plan and try to climb above the overcast, as it would be suicidal to fly any lower.

Steadily, 'B' Baker nosed her way upwards with engines at full bore, striving to break free of the stranglehold of cloud that engulfed her. We were very conscious of being out on a limb, alone in a hostile sky and knew from previous experience the danger of being isolated; German flak could be lethal against a solitary target. So every few seconds we changed course as we climbed. The radar screen was a sea of green, not a blip in sight.

The altimeter needle crept steadily round the dial. At 14,000 the rain-cloud was still as thick as ever, we had no option but to continue upwards, ever upwards. Surely we must break through soon!

# WE BITE THE DUST

I sat tensely by my radio; there was the sound of heavy breathing on the intercom – someone had forgotten to switch his mike off. The Lanc, never exactly famous for its sound-proofing, wasn't too noisy at cruising speed, but when at full revs the merlins really produced a bellow which made the very air vibrate.

George had just changed direction when, without warning, there was a blinding flash followed by an explosion of such violence that I was thrown against the side of the fuselage. Simultaneously came a shout over the intercom which ended abruptly, followed by silence. I jumped to the astro-dome, from where I could see the starboard wing ablaze, with both engines out of action. Our poor Lanc went into a dive and looking up front I could see George wrestling with her like a madman. There was no time for debate; this was it, the dreaded moment we had rehearsed for so often. George yelled "bale out" and as in a nightmare I clipped on my 'chute and picking up a torch, scrambled back along the fuselage, being thrown from side to side as I went. My torch flashed upon the mid-upper turret, it was smashed and poor old Ted was dangling inertly from his harness, lifeless and bespattered with blood. Sickened, I lurched on past him towards the rear door. The beam of light flashed past it to the rear turret and to my horror, there, amid what remained of the rear turret, was Winky, slumped grotesquely over his guns. Having satisfied myself that he was beyond human aid, I turned in desperation to my avenue of escape, the rear door, only to find it jammed; the blast must have distorted the air-frame. There was an axe located nearby and in a frenzy I wrenched it from its mounting and attacked the door, but all to no avail.

As a last resort I turned and fought my way up front, please God let someone still be there! Then I spied George, all alone, still at the controls, looking back and beckoning to me. I shot past him and dived down through the front hatch amazed that I had enough awareness to delay pulling the rip-cord until I was well clear.

The 'chute opened up with a bang and a wrench that threatened to pull me in half – I never did have my harness tight enough! Funny, but when you practice baling out drills, you don't visualise jumping into a black void and hanging, apparently motionless, in ten-tenths cloud, with no way of knowing how near or far away the ground is, or if you are even the right way up!

I remember hoping desperately that George had managed to jump and was aware that, but for me, he would have baled out earlier. I've known lots of chaps who received decorations for simply being lucky enough to complete a tour, but I wonder how many unsung heroes there were whose deeds, like George's, went unobserved and unrewarded; I shudder to contemplate the outcome for me but for his bravery.

The only other tangible thing that I can remember thinking during this hiatus in the clouds was bemoaning the fact that I had left my pipes (the smoking variety) back on board. Some friends had given me a beautiful pair of pre-war briars in a velvet lined case, for my 21st birthday. I was an avid pipe-smoker and the thought of those pipes sitting in the little drawer near my radio equipment brought tears of frustration to my eyes.

A few seconds before I hit the ground, the swirling cloud thinned a little and in the eerie stillness I saw a dull flash in the hazy distance followed by a heavy, muffled thud; our Lanc, which only a few frantic minutes ago had seemed such a sanctuary, winging us home, was no more.

Then everything went black. My next recollection is of feeling a floating sensation, as though I was at the business end of a huge pendulum. Slowly, my wits began to return and the situation began to piece itself together. I was gently swaying from my parachute harness, the canopy was entangled in the foliage above and mother earth, barely visible, was about six feet below. Rain dripped steadily and I was conscious of being soaked to the skin. Gingerly I flexed my arms and legs; surprisingly, they appeared to be in working order. My body felt as though it had lost an argument with a steam roller and I put a hand to my face, to discover that my mouth was considerably larger than I remembered it.

With something of a shock, I realised that dawn was breaking and that as we had been blasted from the sky at about eight p.m., a whole night was unaccounted for. I was by nature a sound sleeper, but this was ridiculous!

Having weighed up my predicament, and prospects not being exactly rosy, I decided to press the release and drop to the ground. No point in hanging around! After consulting my compass and not knowing whether the territory was friendly or hostile (the Allies were pushing East at a rate of knots), I decided to head towards the West, at least it was away from Berlin! The woods seemed endless, trackless and hostile.

Back at home we had received instructions on 'escape' procedure, but the reality was like nothing I had ever visualised. It's hard to picture one's self soaked to the skin, bloodied and concussed, squelching through undergrowth, looking in vain for somewhere to hide up. All the best books on escape strongly advised hiding up by day and travelling by night, so all I had to do was find a nice dry barn with loads of hay; that's what they do in all the spy thrillers.

With this mirage in mind I pressed on and on and on, but there was no Shangri-La, only – "Hult!" The voice was loud, highly charged and gutteral. I froze. From the shadows emerged a menacing figure – I could just discern the coal-scuttle helmet and the levelled rifle. Without speaking, he nudged me in the ribs with his rifle barrel and pointed to a barely visible track, indicating the direction I was to take. There didn't seem to be much point in arguing!

A few yards along the path, we rounded a bend and beheld, in a clearing, a house of imposing proportions, like the chateaux to be seen in holiday brochures. I was marched up the steps, through the front door and into a large hall. There were German soldiers everywhere – I never saw any civilians, although it was evident from the architecture that I was in France, if only just.

They put me into a room that led off the hall. It was sparsely furnished, just a plain table and a couple of chairs. On the wall was a rather fly-blown mirror and one glance gave me the fright of my life. The face I beheld would make Quasi Modo look handsome! It was swollen, with a deep cut in the centre of the forehead; the mouth was about an inch wider than normal, which gave the face a sort of lop-sided leer. There were sundry other cuts and scratches and the whole repulsive visage was liberally coated with congealed blood.

To my immense surprise, a young soldier, whom I presumed to be a medical orderly, appeared with a bowl of water and proceeded, in quite a humane manner to bathe my face and administer antiseptic, closing the cuts with sticking plaster. One enormous piece, applied to my elongated mouth, resulted in half of the orifice itself as well as the wound being closed. It was difficult enough trying to make my captors understand me, but attempting to enunciate through about an inch of mouth didn't exactly help matters. As for smiling – mind you, there wasn't much temptation to do that!

I must confess to being moved by this touch of humanity, more so because it was completely unexpected. After all, I was one of the British murderers who were laying waste the Fatherland. For years the Goebbels propaganda machine had been conducting a hate campaign against us, so any sort of compassion was the last thing to be expected.

After the wash and brush-up, I was apparently deemed to be presentable enough for a spot of interrogation and was escorted into another room, where a typically Prussian-looking Lieutenant sat at a desk. His English being better than my German, it was mutually agreed to conduct the interview in that language. It turned out to be a singularly one-sided affair, as to all the questions I parroted my name, rank and number interminably. Very soon he started to lose his cool and reverting to his native tongue, gave me what I presume was a Teutonic dressing down. I watched fascinated as his complexion turned a vivid puce and little bubbles formed and burst at the corners of his mouth. Then he shouted for a guard, and I was manhandled roughly from his presence, back to the room with the mirror.

Not having eaten since our egg-and-bacon at Spilsby, my stomach was clamouring for sustenance and I tried to convey this to my custodians. Eventually, I was introduced to what I later realised was their normal fare – dark, heavy rye bread, ersatz cheese squeezed from a tooth-paste like tube and ersatz coffee made from nothing that remotely resembled any coffee I had ever tasted. (Later I found that it, along with its tea equivalent, was fractionally better as a smoke than a drink!). However, any old port in a storm – I ate ravenously.

Shortly after I was hustled outside and bundled into the back of a car, the lines of which looked vaguely familiar – it was my introduction to the Volkswagon Beetle. After a few hair-raising minutes we landed up in a small town where once again I was taken to a building of most impressive dimensions – the Wehrmacht certainly looked after its own!

Without preamble I was ushered into the presence of an officer, this time a Hauptman, next to whom sat a civilian. The interview followed a similar pattern to the previous one, only this time, the chap in civvies, presumably Gestapo, assaulted my ear-drums in a very passable English, leaving me in no doubt that if I insisted in my policy of non co-operation, the consequences would indeed be dire. Eventually, the tirade abated; I don't know how long this interrogation had lasted (time does seem to drag a bit on these occasions), but at long last they banished me from their presence and as I left the room under escort, I got the distinct impression that these men did not wish me well!

So far I had seen no-one else from 'our side' and looking at the field grey can become deadly boring. I was desperate for news of the rest of the lads, but refrained from inquiring, as I felt somehow that my curiosity might be used as a lever to extract information from me. It really was amazing to me that, in December of 44, with the Germans in retreat on every front, that they should pursue their policy of subjecting prisoners to lengthy interrogations. Later, I began to understand the German mind and its dedication to excellence, which precludes it from cutting corners and tends to stifle initiative.

My next port of call turned out unexpectedly to be a farm-house. Again I was transported in the 'Beetle' to the edge of town and handed over to an N.C.O. He was, I would judge, in his late thirties, with an impressive row of ribbons. He and his platoon had commandeered the farm, retaining the farmer's wife and daughter to attend to their creature comforts. Most of the soldiers looked unbelievably young, I would have guessed around sixteen. The N.C.O. had a smattering of English, and he told me the town was called Marcolsheim and that he and his lads were waiting to go to the front, which he said was only about ten kilometres away. I cursed my luck – so near and yet so far.

The youngsters, thankfully, looked at me with curiosity rather than animosity, they even went so far as to share their bread and cheese with me. After a day, the like of which I'd never experienced before or since, I was cordially invited to sleep on the floor with my hosts – I needed no second bidding, promptly curling up in a corner, fully clothed, hemmed in by umpteen boy soldiers; if mother could see me now!

Next morning the farm-house was buzzing with activity. The youngsters were diligently cleaning and oiling their small-arms and there was an air of expectancy around the place, accentuated by the exaggerated horse-play in which they indulged. I wasn't quite sure if this was due to highly strung nerves or the desire to impress me – perhaps a bit of both.

Just as I was wondering what was in store for me, the ubiquitous Beetle appeared on the scene and with sinking heart I recognised the smirk on the face of the driver. Twice before he had subjected me to his own particular form of mental and physical torture, driving with such an excess of zeal that I was convinced that, having survived all that the German Army and Mother Nature could throw at me, I was destined to meet my maker as a result of this madman's antics in a Beetle! Now, I saw from the expression on his face, he was going to have a third try, after all, there's nothing like a captive audience!

We rattled, swayed and bucked along roads never intended for motorised traffic, and just as I began to wonder how much more his contraption or I could take, we pulled up with a shriek of brakes inside the courtyard of a large building, which I guessed was the local Gendarmerie. This was confirmed when they herded me into a large room full to overloading with humanity in every shape and form. Having bemoaned the absence of fellow potential escapees, suddenly I couldn't move for them! Most of my fellow internees were French Moroccans, which came as a surprise, as I wasn't aware that they were involved in hostilities.

I scanned the swarthy sea of faces, hoping perhaps to see a face or two just a shade lighter, or even familiar, but drew a blank. Then in desperation I yelled – "Anyone here speak English?" and from the far recesses of the room came a "Yup." With great difficulty I ploughed my way through the seething mass of less than aromatic bodies, in the direction from which this magical mono-syllable had come.

Eventually, I reached its source, and it proved to be a couple of American GIs looking and feeling like the rest of us, very much the worse for wear. They had only been 'in the bag' for a few hours and were kicking themselves for having been 'jumped' while on reconnaissance in a jeep. Having nothing else to do, we talked the hours away. It's amazing how stimulating conversation can be after a word famine and I was transported on visits to the Grand Canyon, Niagara Falls, Hollywood, New York, Washington, the West, the East, the North and the South. They must have had bikes!

In turn I tried to give them a mental picture of the U.K. and its main attractions and was embarrassed to discover just how little I knew of or had seen of my homeland, or perhaps I wasn't very good at romanticising.

When it grew dark, as it does very early in the cold December evenings, I began to wonder where on earth we were all going to sleep, as in the room it was a case of 'standing room only'. No guards were available to ask, so we finished up in a huddle on the floor, propping one another up, with no one having the luxury of lying down. I don't remember much about that night; funny how the mind discards that which is not worthy of remembrance. All my life, though, I have associated times and places with smells – a sort of malodorous filing system. Happily, most of these sensations are more aptly described as fragrances, but I still get a feeling of nausea when I recall that particular 'black hole' and its fetid atmosphere that defied description.

When, after an eternity, dawn broke, there was a sound of great activity outside – the jack-boots were working overtime. Then the doors were flung open and guards with fixed bayonets entered the room and commenced kicking the Moroccans in the most brutal fashion. Anyone showing resistance was given the bayonet and rifle-butt treatment. The two Yanks and I retreated into a corner, trying to make ourselves inconspicuous. Then, to our great surprise and relief, the Moroccans were herded outside into the courtyard, leaving we three alone to stew in that fearful stench. We wondered why on earth we had been exempted from that barbaric display of cruelty. Later we were to learn that there was indeed a reason, perhaps the only one that could account for that 'over the top' display by the guards – it appears that Moroccans don't take prisoners! I often wonder what became of them and why, if it were true, the Germans bothered to take them captive anyway.

The German attitude to us seemed to unbend a trifle after the mass exodus. They even took us into another room while our original one was swilled out like a pig-stye and the floor was strewn with hay – a vast improvement, so that when we returned to it, while not exactly fragrant, at least the stomach didn't heave.

Later that morning there was more commotion outside and in the hubbub we could discern voices other than German. There was no mistaking the quick, staccato lingo of France and bringing broad grins to the faces of my Yankee friends, the slower, rather nasal intonations of what passes for English across the Atlantic.

Dramatically, as though it were a stage setting, the doors swung open and a phalanx of bodies advanced towards us across the room. At least they were friendly and relatively wholesome and the Americans, although total strangers, greeted each other like long-lost brothers. Then, at the back of the crowd, I saw a tall figure in dark blue. I looked as though at a mirage, rubbed my eyes and it still didn't go away – it

41

was George! Never, in all my life have I ever been so glad to see anyone. I shouted his name and he looked at me, at first uncomprehendingly, then as he saw through my sticking plaster disguise, his face, which was thinner than I remembered, very dirty and with about half an inch of black stubble, beamed a smile of recognition, and then we were slapping each other on the back as though we'd just won the War single-handed.

I asked if he had any news of the rest of the lads, and he shook his head sadly. I remarked that it might not be a bad thing, they might be home by now, having a drink at The Bell. This seemed to cheer him up and he told me he had seen Bill, Artie and Eric all bale out. Then I told him the sad news about Ted and Winky; this merely confirmed his worst fears. It was obvious that George took his responsibility as captain of the aircraft very seriously and was very concerned with the welfare of 'his lads', as he invariably called them, even though several of them were many years older than himself.

We felt optimistic that at least some of the crew had made it to freedom, especially as the Allied troops were so near. George said that there was a good chance that Artie would evade capture, as he spoke fluent German.

With the arrival of George, things certainly took a turn for the better. Just before he came my morale was at its lowest ebb; I was very weak and figured that my chances of survival were, to say the least, minimal. But now there was a resurgence of hope, I was no longer a stranger in a strange land. We sat and talked by the hour, of anything and everything – I'd forgotten what a benison conversation can be. Our living conditions were greatly improved, as the new batch of Kriegies was about twenty strong, less than half the size of the Moroccan contingent. There was room to lie down, and it was even permitted to leave the room to attend to the wants of nature.

We had just finished a meal of black bread and soup when the air raid sirens wailed. Shortly after we heard the throb of aero-engines and the sharp crack of light flak. Our only source of daylight was through a narrow horizontal slit window at head height and by standing on tip-toe it was just possible to see out. There was a broad stretch of river, presumably the Rhine, and in the middle distance was the span of an iron bridge. We watched enthralled as American Thunderbolts came screaming down, flying through a hail of flak to dive-bomb the bridge.

A great cheer went up as a bomb found its target and one of the Yanks started a commentary on the proceedings, as though it were an American football game. Time and again the aircraft hurtled down to release their bombs, while others attacked the gun emplacements with machine-gun fire. Several more hits were scored and in the few minutes that the raid lasted, the bridge was reduced to a mass of twisted metal.

Having a grand-stand seat at this impeccable display of dive-bombing did us all a power of good, just when we were sorely in need of a morale booster. Predictably, though, it had the reverse effect on our gaolers, who seemed to hold us personally responsible for what, from their point of view, was a debacle. We decided it was best to try and humour them and knowing the German temperament, this wasn't exactly easy.

Two more days went by, with nothing to relieve the boredom. There was much speculation as to what, in view of the Allied advance, would become of us. One consensus of opinion, freely aired by the pessimists among us, was that we should all be shot out of hand, while others pooh-poohed this macabre suggestion, maintaining that it was in the interests of the Jerries to treat us leniently, as very soon the boot would be on the other foot and reprisals could be very painful.

As a consequence to all this conjecture, when, in the dark of early morning, we were awakened with shouts of 'Raus, Raus' and hustled outside into the courtyard, our befuddled brains were in torment and we half expected to be confronted with a firing squad. So it was with considerable relief that we were marched down the road. After only a few minutes the lack of exercise and food started to take its toll and just as we were beginning to wilt, we arrived at a railway siding. It had been raining steadily, in fact, since my untimely arrival it seldom seemed to do anything else. We were shepherded into a large barn-type building, presumably to await a train. It was common knowledge that 'train-busting' was a very popular sport among the boys of Fighter Command and that railway services would inevitably be disrupted. Nevertheless, after a wait of about six hours, we embarked upon a train for a journey that still makes me shudder when I think about it.

At first sight the carriages looked quite presentable (we had been expecting goods wagons), except that they were completely windowless and bore a few other scars of battle. The seats were of slatted wood and any form of heating was non-existent. As soon as we got under way, the wind and driving rain beat in upon us unmercrfully. We huddled pathetically together, wondering if perhaps we were being subjected to this prolonged torture in lieu of a firing squad. Perhaps they were saving bullets and that at journeys end we should all be shoveled out like so much offal!

We progressed in a series of stops and starts. Once we heard aero-engines and the sound of cannon-fire. Who on earth could be flying in this atrocious weather?

Luckily, our mobile refrigerator sustained no further damage, although as we continued that nightmare journey, we saw many shattered, burnt out engines and wagons reduced to matchwood. As darkness fell, our stuttering progress finally ran out of steam and it was with enormous relief that we were ordered to bestir our numbed bodies and get off the train. Painfully we clambered down, not caring where we were; anything was better than that hell-upon-wheels.

Our guards had located a large barn and we needed no second bidding. It was dry and had an earthen floor strewn with hay. Luxury is a relative thing and soon we were wallowing in our new environment, trying to get the blood coursing through our veins again by massaging and getting as much exercise as our restricted circumstances would allow. No sooner, it seemed, had we sunk into a stupefied sleep than the now familiar 'Raus Raus' dragged us protestingly back to reality. We were, it appears, to resume our conducted tour of Germany. After all, the Rhineland was famous for its scenery and fairy-tale castles!

Our worst fears were allayed as soon as the barn door opened – the interminable rain had ceased and to give our sagging spirits a much-needed boost, when we entrained it was into a carriage that actually sported windows. The rate of progress, however, was about the same as the previous day. I remember seeing two large areas of devastation, which someone said were Karlsruhr and Damstadt, towns of the industrial Ruhr that had taken a fearful battering. We gained no satisfaction in witnessing this end product of aerial bombardment, just a feeling of despair at the utter futility of it all.

Eventually, we puffed and snorted our way into Frankfurt station, which, although somewhat battered, was still functional. We stood huddled in a bedraggled, forlorn little group on the platform. The place was seething with activity, the sort of orderly chaos to be seen at innumerable main-line stations. Then we were spotted by a group of youths, who started shouting abuse, which seemed to be directed particularly at George and I – we were the only ones dressed in blue, not exactly in our favour in this neck of the woods. Then suddenly the air was thick with empty beer bottles (at least I presume they were empty). We instinctively ducked to try and evade the onslaught, but I think my reflexes were a little on the slow side, as one of the bottles scored a bulls-eye on my forehead and everything went black. I came to on the floor, with George's be-whiskered face gazing down upon me, full of concern. The missile had re-opened an existing cut and but for a little blood and bruising, I was soon little the worse for wear. The mob had dispersed; I suppose the sight of me poleaxed had sated their appetite for revenge, at least temporarily. We learned subsequently that Frankfurt had been subjected to a mauling by Bomber Command the previous night, so it was no wonder the hounds were baying for blood. They naturally concluded that George and I had been directly involved.

We spent the night in a subway beneath the station; it was there that I had an insight into the German mentality. There were toilets down below and I marvelled at their cleanliness. Up above was chaos and destruction, but down there all was spick and span and I watched entranced as an elderly toilet attendant religiously polished the copper and brass-work, not even bothering to glance at this motley horde that had invaded his realm, sullying his pristine floor with their muddy boots. Somehow I couldn't visualise a similar situation at London's Waterloo!

Next morning we entrained yet again, for an unknown destination. The whole area was laid waste and the atmosphere was one of grey desolation, with people moving around like zombies. Shortly after leaving Frankfurt we had a second taste of 'train-busting'. Once again there was the sudden roar of engines, that crash of cannon fire and the terrier-like barking of the light flak with which all the trains seemed to be equipped. Again we bore charmed lives and came through unscathed. Who knows, perhaps we were destined to die in our beds after all. It really would have been ironic to have fallen victim to our own guns in an alien land.

Eventually, we detrained at a small station and were marched up a steep, gravelled road to what, from outward appearances looked like a well-organised military establishment, except that it was hemmed in by a barbed wire fence of ridiculous proportions. These Jerries didn't trust anyone! On enquiry we were told that the name of the town was Limburg and with a feeling of relief we marched into the camp compound. There were POWs everywhere, but as far as I could see they all seemed to be wearing either khaki or olive-green. Sure enough, George and I were segregated from the rest, who, as they were chaperoned away, turned and waved and we wished each other well. After all, we were quite intimate friends, having been on cuddling terms on the first never-to-be-forgotten leg of our journey.

We hung around the office, while innumerable 'phone calls' were made. Didn't anyone want us? Apparently something had gone wrong with the documentation –

how very un-Germanic! We asked if we might be permitted to have a shower before continuing our sojourn, but our request was greeted with emphatic shakes of the head, which means the same in any language. However, we were given a little sustenance – yes, you've guessed it – black bread, tooth-paste cheese and that fantastic concoction they had the effrontery to call coffee.

It began to get dark and we had thoughts of spending the night there, after all it was safer than being on the railway. But they had other plans and soon we were plodding off down the road with two armed guards. One of them was a dapper little chap who possessed something that was in very short supply at that time – a smile. In fact, when you addressed him, although he didn't understand a word, he positively beamed. His companion, however, was the complete opposite: a big, heavy-jowled brute with a surly disposition, who handled his rifle as though longing to use it on us. George and I agreed to treat the latter with kid gloves.

This time the train took us back the way we had come and our frustration knew no bounds when after the type of journey we had now come to expect, we landed up in Frankfurt Station once more. This time, thank God, there was no reception committee, as it was dawn and the place was almost deserted. We were prodded in the direction of another platform, where we settled down to await another train. Rail travel, German style in 1944 was not for the faint hearted, as it entailed endless waiting, detours (it was quite normal to be shunted into a siding for half a day or so) and of course, there was the ever present threat from above.

Eventually, another steam-hissing monster backed into the station and soon, with the escort we had dubbed Laurel and Hardy, we were on our way again. We had long ceased to be concerned as to where we might be going. It would be nice to have an inkling of what fate may have in store, but after all, we were being treated to a scenic tour of the Third Reich, with all expenses paid!

This trip, however, turned out to be mercifully brief, although if we had known what was in store for us – but then I suppose everyone thinks that way many times during their life.

Our destination turned out to be a place called Dulag Luft, which was an Air Crew Interrogation Centre. First impressions were quite favourable. The place looked clean and orderly and we saw quite a few RAF types, but no familiar faces. Once again we asked if we might shower and shave. They vetoed the shower, but presented us with a safety razor apiece, complete with much used rusty blade. Armed with these and cold water only, we attacked our stubbly beards, but the process was so painful I wish I'd never started. We finished looking like fugitives from a chain gang.

Next we were subjected to a thorough search, surprisingly the first time this had happened and were put into solitary cells. Most of the German staff spoke English, and we were told that we should not be detained for more than a couple of days at the most. At first sight my cell looked almost attractive, in a Spartan sort of a way. It had a large central heating radiator – very impressive, as well as a bed with an admittedly thin mattress and a couple of threadbare blankets, which represented luxury compared to the conditions we had recently encountered.

But, not surprisingly, all was not as it seemed. Their ploy was to have the radiator going full blast all day, so that you were dripping with sweat and then at night no heat at all, so that the unfortunate inmate would shiver with the cold of a December night, precluding any hope of sleep. I was subjected to this softening up process for two days and nights, before being dragged in a stupor before an interrogator. He was a Luftwaffe pilot, sporting an impressive row of ribbons on his chest and with a charming suave manner. He started the interview with the good news that Bill and Eric were safe. From then on things deteriorated as he started turning the screw and after the usual 'bully and threat' routine, I was led back to my cell to stew.

I can't dwell for long on the rest of our stay at the Dulag Luft Rest Home. Suffice it to say that it was just about the longest week of my life thus far. The interviews continued daily, together with the 'hot and cold' treatment, so that when they finally gave up I was tottering with fatigue. Finally, I was taken from my cell and led out into a yard, where there were several Air Crew Bod's, all looking just about as ghastly as I undoubtedly was. To my delight George soon joined the party. Before Heilbronn he had been a massive fifteen-stoner, although admittedly he could have done with losing a few pounds. But the privations of the last fortnight had really taken their toll, obviously the compulsory crash course in slimming didn't suit his constitution and his hollow eyes and sunken cheeks were testimony to this. His spirit, however, was unbroken and when one of the guards, who was arrogant even by German standards, started to throw his weight around and tried to intimidate us, I saw the light of battle come into George's eyes. If he hadn't been restrained, that guard would have been very much the worse for wear and so, of course, would George.

We were a group of about a dozen, and stood chatting while our Prussian overlords decided what to do and when to do it. Curiously, one of our chaps, a very boyish looking navigator, told me he had been shot down on the Frankfurt raid the night before I had failed to dodge the beer bottle. I showed him the battle scar on my forehead and told him how I had come by it. He laughed and didn't seem a bit contrite, even when I pointed out that I had been punished for his wrong-doing.

Eventually (why did everything take so long?) we were marched off back to the railway. Why they bothered with an armed guard I don't know, as we didn't have enough strength left to raise a smile between us and surely those guns could be better employed on the Russian Front!

As usual, rumours were rife as to our destination as we progressed in the now familiar grasshopper manner. Never again would we criticise the old Southern and Great Western back home, but in view of the awful hammering it had taken, it was a miracle that the German railway system was able to function even sporadically.

The trouble with this mode of travel was that you were kept guessing. Every time the train stopped you wondered – is this it? At last our curiosity was satisfied when we landed up near a town called Wetzlar. It was a transit camp run by the Red Cross and for the first time since leaving England we were treated like hurnan beings. With what, by recent comparison, was red carpet treatment, we were fed with a nourishing stew before being led to the showers; our clothes were fumigated and then, best of all, we were allowed to sleep the clock around.

For three whole days we were feted at the Wetzlar holiday camp. The staff of the International Red Cross was simply superb. I knew the organisation had a record of which to be proud, but hadn't realised that in fact they were the nearest thing to miracle makers to hit this planet in almost 2000 years! From being dirty, weak, bedraggled automatons we were transformed into passable representatives of the human race. The most important things the Red Cross gave us were pride and, above all, hope.

On our third day there I got into a conversation with one of the staff, a Swede and told him about the 'hot and cold' torture dished out at Dulag Luft. He smiled sadly and said that they had known for ages about that despicable practice, but, as their occasional visits were never unheralded, it was never possible to catch our German friends in the act – but they were still trying.

All good things must come to an end and our little group was told to prepare to resume our former nomadic wanderings, by courtesy of the German railway system. We marched away to the nearby station looking almost spruce, unrecognisable from the disreputable, evil-smelling bunch of a few days ago. As usual, our destination was kept a well-guarded secret, but we knew there were few Stalags in Western Germany, so were resigned to a long, although not necessarily tedious journey.

In the event, it turned out to be something of a marathon. Three days and nights of it, this was the real scenic job, as we puffed and panted our weary way from one scene of devastation to another. The Fatherland was so obviously tottering on the brink, with the populace going dazedly through the motions of existence. I recall vividly when we stopped at a small town. Looking out of the train window we saw an old man with a horse and cart. The horse, bony and dejected, had obviously dug his heels in, refusing to budge and the man was whiplashing him in a frenzy of rage. Had that occurred in England, I have no doubt that the chap would have been given short shrift, but here no-one bothered to raise an eyebrow, let alone a hand. How much this reflected the German attitude towards animals I don't know, but I would hate to think the lethargy displayed at this act of blatant cruelty was the norm.

Time and again as we wended our way deeper and deeper into Hitler's Third Reich, we saw the wrecks, some still smouldering, of engines, carriages and wagons lying near to the track and wondered, by the law of averages, how long it would be before ours suffered a similar fate. But we seemed to lead a charmed life; true, there were several alarms and once another train was strafed as it passed us going in the opposite direction – it was hit and obviously in some distress. Our driver didn't hang around to see the outcome, but bolted into a tunnel and there we stayed, choked by smoke and fumes for about half an hour, when it was judged safe to emerge.

Our food rations during this seemingly never-ending journey were non-existent, and depended entirely on what our guards could scrounge whenever and wherever we stopped, which was frequently. Again, black bread and ersatz cheese appeared to be the staple diet – the country seemed to run on it. Often it was a case of grab what you can when you can, and at this George was far more proficient than I, being larger and having longer arms! Without him the pangs of hunger would have been much more severe.

*Winthorpe, June 1944*
*Back row: 'Winky' Turner (R/G), George Wall (Pilot), Roy Hill (WOp/AG)*
*Front row: Eric Dunn (F/E), 'Jock' Sweeney (M/U), Artie Clarke (Nav), Bill Wulff (B/A)*

## POST OFFICE TELEGRAM

Charges to pay
s.
d.

RECEIVED

No.

OFFICE STAMP

FLEET
ALDERSHOT
5 DEC. 44
HANTS.

To

Prefix.   Time handed in.   Office of Origin and Service Instructions.   Words.

1.12 p.m   11.33 - SIK F/T    OHMS   75

From ACH BPW

Priority Mr S. A. Hill 135 Albert Street Fleet Hants

Deeply regret to inform you that your son 157919 F/o Roy Ernest Hill was reported missing as a result of air operations on the night 4th December 1944 stop letter

B or C

Wt 20815 9/43 Orch. St.

# Dulag-Luft Germany

Date __13.12.44__

I have been taken prisoner of war in Germany. I am in good health — ~~slightly wounded~~ (cancel accordingly).

We will be transported from here to another Camp within the next few days. Please don't write until I give new address.

Kindest regards

Christian Name and Surname: _Roy Hill_

Rank: _Flying Officer_

_R.A.F._

Detachment: _____

*Sent from Dulag Luft. The only communication received in U.K.*

# POST OFFICE

## TELEGRAM

Charges to pay

s. _____ d. _____

RECEIVED

m _____ m

From _____

Prefix. | Time handed in. | Office of Origin and Service Instructions. | Words.

4.34 | London Telex 75

No. _____

OFFICE STAMP

19 JAN. 45

To _____ m

O H M S

CC JA Hill Esq 135 & West St Fleet St

From Air Ministry 74 Oxford St W.1.

P.C.114 19/1/45 the name of your son

F/O Roy Ernest Hill was included in a

German broadcast on 18/1/45 as prisoner

Stop you are advised to wait the

For free repetition of doubtful words telephone "TELEGRAMS ENQUIRY" or call, with this form at office of delivery. Other enquiries should be accompanied by this form and if possible, the envelope

B or C

Wt 20815 9/43 Orch. Sc.

# POST OFFICE TELEGRAM

**Charges to pay**
s. .......... d. ..........

**RECEIVED**

From ..........

Prefix.   Time handed in.   Office of Origin and Service Instructions.   Words.

No. ..........
**OFFICE STAMP**

To ..........

m .......... m

information with receive pending official confirmation stop any further ... will be immediately forwarded to you stop treat of hardcase being posted stop

1351A

*Major Friedrich-Karl Müller, Officer Commanding I/NJGII*

*George, 1944 – my saviour*

*My best Christmas pose – 1944*

*The Old Custom House, Marcolsheim – scene of my incarceration*

MY FRIEND IVAN

*I wonder if he's still smiling?*

# CHAPTER EIGHT

# STALAG LIFE

So finally, just two days before Christmas 1944, the long, long trek ended at Stalag Luft I, situated near a little town called Barth, right up on the Baltic coast in what until recently was East Germany. For one ghastly moment, as we entered the main gates, I thought that our hosts had made yet another faux pas, as apart from the guards, the only uniforms in evidence were American. We were soon to find out, however, that Yanks comprised 90% of the inmates, the other 10% being made up of Aussies, New Zealanders, Canadians, Rhodesians, South Africans and Poles, as well as the U.K. contingent. We were shepherded into the British compound, which had its own entity. The Senior British Officer was a Group Captain Weir, who strangely, was not Air Crew. It appears he was something of a back-room boffin specialising in bomb design and had been shot down and taken prisoner whilst on a flight observing the behaviour of one of his progeny!

Having been allocated a room in a barrack block, George and I entered, and I was irnmediately greeted with – "Hi there, Roy!" Having no idea my fame had preceded me, I glanced in the direction of the voice and there, sitting on a top bunk, swinging his legs and grinning hugely, was a familiar face, unseen for several years. I had known Eddie Smith back home in Fleet. He was a couple of years my senior and had quite a reputation as a middle-weight amateur boxer. I, at one time, had aspirations in that direction myself (until I was pulverised by a human bean-pole at Madley) and Eddie was something of a hero to me. I lost sight of him when he joined the RAF in the early stages of War, but followed his meteoric rise in the local paper. He was a F/Lt. Air Gunner, sporting the D.F.C. and had been 'in the bag' for a couple of years or so. Like most of the veterans, he looked in far better shape than we new arrivals, which in itself was encouraging. Perhaps we should get something better to eat than bread and cheese!

I introduced George to Eddie and the latter took us on a conducted tour of the block. The rooms were all identical, containing four pairs of bunk beds and a set of lockers, which were really quite superfluous, as the only worldly goods we possessed we were wearing.

There were two vacant beds in one room (we didn't inquire about the previous occupants) and George and I grabbed them. Our fellow room-mates, who happened to be home at the time, were made up of three more Aussies, two English lads and a Pole. Over the next few months we were going to get to know one another pretty well, unavoidable in those claustrophobic conditions.

One of the Aussies was 'Digger' Hassall, a tough, chunky RAF Regiment type. When asked how he came to be a POW, not being Air Crew, he merely said that he hadn't run fast enough! He was a very important member of the Stalag community, being self-appointed camp trader; there was even a lock on his locker! However he managed it I never knew, but without a word of German (except the epithets, which everyone knew), he could conjure up all manner of unlikely items from the outside world.

When we first arrived, prisoners were still getting the occasional Red Cross parcel, but the supply soon dried up. One of the ingredients of these 'manna from heaven' parcels was bars of vitamin chocolate, known as 'D' bars, which were used as camp currency. Digger used these, in addition to tobacco and cigarettes to bargain with 'The Goons' and as parcels grew scarcer, so the value of our chocolate currency increased dramatically until, by April 1945, lOUs to the value of 50 pounds were tendered in payment for one bar. Right up to the end, old Digger continued to produce 'D' bars with Houdini-like mystique. If only half his lOUs were honoured, he would be a very rich man. I wonder if he ever found it necessary to work for a living after the war?

Another personality worthy of mention was the Pole. Alex Delage was a member of an all Polish crew. Their Wimpey had been shot down by a German night fighter; they all baled out safely and were uninjured, landing up at Barth together. However, they were in dispute, as each blamed the others for their fall from grace. So great was their animosity towards one another that they refused to live together, insisting on being in five different rooms, a situation I just can't visualise ever happening to our lads.

Alex was a member of the intelligentsia and was a mine of information on almost everything. As well as English and Polish, he spoke French, German and Russian. Towards the War's end when it became evident that the Russians were almost certainly going to have the privilege of liberating us, Alex taught us a few phrases of Russian – just in case. He would speak a sentence or two, and we would write it down phonetically and then learn it in parrot fashion. So – *'Onee Myee Tovarischee'* became – *'These are my friends'* and *'Ya Angleesky Lotchic'* meant *'I am an English Officer'* and so on. In all he taught us about fifteen of them. Later I tried them out on a guerilla fighter and was amazed when he understood me.

Alex was much travelled, having fled Poland when the Germans first invaded and as a memento he gave me a map he had drawn on which his wanderings are depicted. I still have it and when occasionally I take it from the drawer and dust it off, I get a mental picture of Alex, sitting Buddha-like on his top bunk, smoking his evil-smelling pipe and philosophising to us, his captive audience.

The day following our arrival another batch of Kriegies came in and among them was a gaunt, disheveled Bill Wulff. He had always had something of a lean and hungry look, but now his face was positively cadaverous and his tattered uniform hung loosely over his shrunken frame. It was obvious he had been through the mill, but Bill, never very voluble, drew a veil over the experiences of the last three weeks. Nothing, he said, had happened that he would ever wish to recall. George and I felt concerned, not so much at his physical condition, but at the rather haunted, hopeless expression in his eyes. I wondered how much Dulag Luft was responsible for that – they had much to answer for. Bill had seen nothing of the rest of the crew, and seemed to perk up a little when we told him Eric was safe.

Suddenly Christmas was upon us and certainly it was like nothing experienced either before or since. The Goons, as we irreverently referred to our Germanic hosts, seemed hyper-active. The war had swung completely in favour of the Allies and Goebbels had taken to threatening and cajoling the populace, warning them of the terrible fate that would be theirs if the Fatherland was to fall. The radio announcers spelled out graphically what would happen if the barbaric marauders from the east were not halted. In truth, the Germans had exacted a terrible toll on the defenceless villages of Russia earlier in the War and now the time of reckoning was at hand. As you sow . . .

As a result of this, many of the prison camp guards seemed to act almost benevolently towards us – I suppose we represented the lesser of two evils. Nevertheless, as we lay in bed on Christmas Eve night, we could hear the dogs sniffing beneath the floor, while in the background from the American compound came an off-key rendering of Silent Night, interspersed with Apache war whoops – some not very bright aviators were celebrating Christmas prematurely. We knew that some illicit, home-made hooch was going to be circulated on Christmas Day; trust the Yanks to jump the gun!

Then from outside came the familiar crunch of jack-boots, as a platoon of the Wermacht marched towards the sound of ribaldry. We held our breath and listened. The discordant singing continued, then just as the voices started to climb at the end of – 'sleep in heavenly pe-ace' – two shots rang out. The carol ceased abruptly in mid-note and the Apaches in mid-whoop. There followed a portentous silence punctuated by the barking of the dogs.

The following morning, Christmas Day, we were all agog to find out about the events of the previous night, but it all turned out to be a bit of a damp squib. Apparently, the shots had merely been fired into the air as a warning and our American cousins had promptly gone to ground, and stayed there.

Christmas morning was cold and bright and I went for a stroll around the compound, gazing longingly beyond the barbed wire at the world beyond. The camp was situated on a sandy peninsula jutting out into the Baltic. In other circumstances, the view might be said to be idyllic, but quite near to the Stalag, the Germans had constructed a military establishment which was in fact a Flak School, where Luftwaffees (the German equivalent to our Waafs) were instructed in the art of destroying aircraft from the ground. The cadets were to be seen drilling on the parade ground, and marching around in little groups, singing their interminable marching songs, largely, I imagine, for our benefit.

My companion on this walk was Mitch, a Canadian Spitfire pilot from our block who I came to know quite well. The Red Cross had supplied us with Log Books and as I hadn't yet written anything in mine, Mitch said he knew a poem, written by a chap named McGee, whom he had known on the squadron; in fact, he had been killed before Mitch himself had been shot down. The poem was called High Flight and he quoted it to me, verbatim, and I wrote it on a scrap of paper, later writing it into my Log Book. The words were most moving and it was not until many years later I was to discover that High Flight was an accepted classic.

Later that morning there was a carol service held in the large hut that served as a church. The camp padre was yet another Mitchell, a New Zealander, held in great esteem by one and all. Captured very early in the war, he, as a non-combatant, could have been repatriated, but preferred to stay and minister the POWs. Padre Mitchell was, to my mind, a hero in the true sense of the word.

In the traumatic atmosphere of a prison camp, when one's mortality is such a tenuous thing, depending on the whims of politicians and dictators, not to mention Camp Commandants, it is perhaps not surprising that men of all creeds and denominations and also those with no religious persuasion, turn instinctively to a Supreme Being for support and comfort. So the church was packed to overflowing and all the familiar carols were sung with great gusto. There we were, singing of peace on earth and goodwill towards men, against a back-drop of barbed wire and menacing 'posten' boxes manned by trigger-happy Krauts. To celebrate Christmas, two of the Aussies in our room, Eric Green and Johnnie Evans, had concocted a Kriegie Cake, made from the hoarded ingredients of Red Cross parcels. I can't say it was the best I have ever tasted, but it helped create something of a festive atmosphere, especially when the promised bottle of 'something special' was smuggled in. The hooch, made largely from raisins and prunes from parcels, was clear as gin and twice as fiery. The effect on our under-nourished constitutions was dramatic to say the least. It had been distilled with an ingenious still made of dried milk tins and to have achieved this without the Germans' knowledge was something of a triumph.

Gradually, as a result of our home-made fire-water, the sounds of revelry began to erupt around the camp, the somewhat muted tones emanating from the British compound being drowned by the sounds as of a John Wayne western coming from the much larger Yankee barracks. Thankfully, Jerry was feeling charitable, or perhaps there was an element of self-preservation creeping in, so, although we kept a weather eye on the Posten boxes, the machine-guns which forever menaced, were silent. So Christmas 1944 passed into the history books peacefully, on a cautious note of hope.

As the New Year dawned, we began adjusting to camp routine. Our main priority was to get and keep as physically and mentally fit as possible. As the Allied and Russian forces ground relentlessly forward, from West and East, we knew that a forced march in either direction was a distinct possibility; we were but pawns in the war game. Unfortunately, the supply of Red Cross parcels dried up, and it was impossible to keep up one's strength on Jerry rations alone. These were meagre at the best and for the last few months of hostilities amounted to rye bread and a concoction masquerading under the name of stew. The one vegetable of which there was a relative abundance was the swede and its taste permeated everything to the point of nausea.

We spent hours plodding around the perimeter fence and as food grew shorter we could feel our strength waning and the ever-present fear of a forced march became something of an obsession. Sometimes we would see spiralling vapour trails climbing vertically in the distance as the Germans test-fired their rockets from Peenemunde and we squirmed with frustration, thinking of the havoc being wrought by the V2s on London and Southern England.

In order to keep dry rot from attacking our brains, we organised discussions on every subject under the sun and anyone who had anything remotely interesting to expound was encouraged to do so. The only subjects barred were service exploits, as 'line-shooting' was regarded as un-British and was severely frowned upon. The vast majority of us were not service regulars, coming from all walks of life and different backgrounds. We had lectures on such divergent subjects as English Law and bird watching, car racing, poaching and deep-sea diving. For my part I managed to talk for about twenty minutes on the Schneider Trophy and its history, which from childhood had fascinated me.

As food got shorter, we found ourselves pre-occupied, indeed obsessed with the subject of food and drink, but food in particular. Foolishly we would draw up great menus of our favourite nosh and swapped addresses of restaurants back home, with notes on their specialties. As a form of self-inflicted torture it would be hard to surpass.

One day I tackled George and Bill with regard to a certain 'Beer Drinkers Challenge Cup.' I felt concerned, as it was among my personal effects back at Spilsby and I could just imagine the look of consternation and disbelief on my Mum's face, should she ever see it. They assured me that Bill, as I had long suspected, had been the 'culprit', he always could drink the rest of us under the table!

CHAPTER NINE

# MY FRIEND IVAN

Following the disastrous mass escape from Stalag Luft 3, with its awful after-math of executions, we were officially forbidden to indulge in that time-honoured pastime of POWs tunnel digging. Nevertheless, beneath the surface of our camp was a veritable labyrinth of defunct tunnels, resembling a gigantic rabbit warren, the legacy of years of industrious tunnelling by the inmates. One of the aforesaid tunnels was instrumental in an incident, which, despite the intervening years, is still indelibly inscribed on my mind. It all came about in the following manner:

Although the camp was for commissioned personnel, there were some Russian other ranks, who performed the most menial tasks and were treated with great severity by their Prussian overlords. One such unfortunate was a character rejoicing in the good old Russian name of Ivan Ivanovitch. He was often to be seen about the place, always very industrious, always with an ear-splitting grin on his face. His sunny personality seemed to transcend all barriers of rank and language and many a despondent POW was given a psychological lift by the mere sight and demeanor of our Russian friend.

Most demeaning of all Ivan's jobs was latrine emptying. Sanitary arrangements were very crude, they were virtually communal earth closets. He had the revolting task of ladling the latrines contents into what, in effect, was a huge rusting metal cylinder, mounted on a wooden chassis with iron-rimmed wheels. The contraption was pulled by a large bony cart-horse. When loaded, the routine was for Ivan to drive his odiferous charge to the camp gates, pick up an armed escort and disappear into the distance, as the hero does in all the best Western films.

It so happened that one morning, as I was taking my constitutional around the perimeter fence, a familiar, awful stench pervaded my nostrils. I turned to trace its source and there, plodding majestically across the Sports Field (a grassless area of compacted sand) like a galleon in full sail, came Ivan and his equipage, en route from the latrine block to the main gate. He sat regally on the driving seat, face beaming, as though he was driving the State Coach.

Then slowly, inexorably, the vehicle and its driver began to sink from view, into one of the old tunnel workings. It sank and sank, until all that was left above ground-level was Ivan's head and shoulders, the grin widening by the minute. It all happened in complete silence and it was uncannily like watching one of the old silent films.

Within seconds, a guard in one of the Posten boxes spotted Ivan's fall from grace and in next to no time, several of his heavily armed friends were on the scene, saw immediately the futility of trying to resolve the situation unaided and retired to have a re-think.

Their next ploy was to bring on a farm tractor, hitch up to the horse and try and pull the ensemble out of the hole, whilst coaxing the nag to aid and abet them. This merely resulted in even more of the old tunnel collapsing, so they brought a load of heavy planking and improvised a ramp. After two hours of frustration, involving several more cave-ins, they finally brought Ivan and his lethal load back to terra firma, to the accompaniment of cheers from the Kriegies, some of whom had helped to dig that tunnel. As for Ivan, he was cheered all the way to the main gate and he responded by bowing and waving in the Royal manner.

A couple of days after Ivan's redolent adventure, a new batch of Kriegies arrived, an all too frequent event. Always we scanned the sea of faces with mixed emotions, hoping perhaps to catch sight of some familiar face that would provide a link with home and all the magic that word conjured up, while at the same time not wishing on anyone else the fate that had befallen you.

On this particular occasion, I had viewed a new intake with no signs of recognition and had returned to the Spartan simplicity of our barrack room, when there was a polite knock on the door. When opened it revealed a stocky figure in RAF blue, surmounted by a ruddy face that was a lattice-work of partly healed lacerations. Not until the apparition smiled did I have a clue as to his identity. The grin revealed a quite exceptional set of molars, which were the trademark of only one person of my acquaintance – Ron Winton, a WOp/AG and friend, last seen about a month before at Spilsby.

I was most curious, as the last time I had seen Ron he had been a Flight Sergeant. Now, just a few weeks later he stood before me, very battered and tattered, but undeniably a fully fledged Pilot Officer. It appears his commission had come through just a few days after I bit the dust.

Naturally, I assumed that his injuries, which were entirely facial, had been received as a result of Luftwaffe ministrations. When I tackled him about them, he seemed a little reluctant to talk, but after a bit of persuasion he unfolded his story, which, to say the least, was anything but run-of-the-mill.

It appears that Ron and his crew had been shot down by a German night-fighter, following an attack on the battleship Lutzow at Gdynia. They had ditched in the Baltic and after nine hours in the dinghy had been picked up by a German air/sea rescue vessel. The mid-upper gunner, a Canadian, had an arm injury, but the rest of the crew came through unscathed.

At this point in the narrative he hesitated, shuffling from foot to foot, obviously and mysteriously embarrassed, although with his face liberally daubed with yellow antiseptic, it was impossible to see if he was blushing. Then, rather haltingly, lowering his voice to a barely audible whisper, he said: "Well, Roy, it was like this. They had taken the injured gunner to hospital (he had his right forearm amputated, and was later repatriated). We had said cheerio to the N.C.O.s who finished up somewhere in Poland and the pilot (F/Lt. John White) and myself were en route to Barth in a train. Rail travel, as you well know, could be quite a hair-raising experience, with so many train-busters lurking around and our progress, with numerous delays and shuntings, was pitifully slow. Anyway, it so happened that just when the train began to gather speed, I wanted to go to the toilet. As I stood there in the little compartment, relieving myself, the train driver suddenly slammed on his brakes and before I could raise my arms in self-defence, I was catapulted forward, the old face crashing straight into a mirror mounted on the wall. The mirror smashed and – well, you can see the result for yourself!"

I most certainly could. Poor old Ron looked so dejected and his obviously true account of events (after all, it's not the sort of story you would concoct, is it?) seemed so ludicrous that I had a job keeping a straight face. Then he looked at me appealingly and said: "But what on earth am I going to tell the folks back home?"

It was good having Ron around. We had always 'hit it off' at Spilsby, being on the same wave-length, and took up where we had left off. He was full of optimism and future prospects seemed quite rosy with him around. His face healed in remarkably quick time, except for the nose, which, for obvious geographical reasons had taken most stick. I'm afraid the scars would always be there to remind him of the day he lost an argument with a looking-glass!

The months of January and February seemed interminable, with sub-zero temperatures and the seemingly endless dark nights. We were losing in the battle for fitness, as rations became even more meagre. The 'stew' got thinner and thinner, they even seemed to be running out of swedes! Our bread allocation amounted to one loaf of rye bread per day for the eight of us. We discovered that, with very precise cutting, it could be divided into 32 wafer-thin slices, four for each of us. For some obscure reason I was deemed to be the most proficient at this exacting task. It was somewhat unnerving having to painstakingly saw away, watched intently by seven pairs of eyes, ensuring that justice was done.

Rumour followed rumour, and we were haunted by the spectre of a forced march, knowing that should this occur, our chances of survival in our present weakened condition were very slim.

As the Allies pressed relentlessly forward from the west and the Russian steam-roller ground remorselessly towards us from the east, tension within the camp increased daily and the frustration of having to sit, awaiting events over which we had no control, began taking its toll.

Strangely, the ones who seemed to be least affected were the old hands, some of whom had been shot down during the faraway days of 1939/40, flying such archaic types as Fairy Battles, Whitleys and Hampdens. After about five years of incarceration, having their hopes raised and dashed so many times, they seemed resigned to letting history take care of itself. Also they seemed to be least affected by the food shortage, no doubt because their diet, prior to the drastic reductions, had never been adequate, so the change was less dramatic.

We were fortunate in being able to get news of the progress made by the Allied army, by means of a radio set, which was secreted under the improvised pulpit in the hut which served as a church. Amazingly, Jerry never did locate this set and daily the news highlights were passed around verbatim. The difference between the reports of the BBC Overseas Service and the official German communique's couldn't have been more contrasting, in fact you would have thought they were commenting on two entirely different conflicts. It was with great difficulty that we suppressed smiles when reading the German version, as displayed on the notice boards, so 'bent' was the truth.

Naturally, we were desperately hoping that when the end came, we would be liberated by forces from the West. We had visions of Monty's tanks suddenly appearing with guns thundering, followed closely by Gaumont British News cameras to record for posterity our historic release.

At long last, winter began to ease its relentless grip, just as our fuel supply was exhausted, with apparently no more forthcoming. It had been impossible to generate any degree of warmth during the latter days of February and eventually even the majority of wooden bed slats had been sacrificed in order to produce a little life saving heat. Sleeping as I did on the top bunk became quite a hazardous procedure, as the pieces of wood supporting my body reduced from ten to a bare minimum of four. George, down below, suffered a number of near misses when I just managed to prevent myself from being dumped unceremoniously onto his recumbent form.

Surprisingly, the influx of POWs seemed, during this period of Allied advance, to accelerate. Obviously the Luftwaffe was far from being a spent force. The vast majority of 'new boys' were Americans, who seemed to arrive in droves. It is true that camp personnel was predominantly Yankee and also with their larger crews (flying Forts and Liberators operated usually with ten crew members) the number of survivors would be higher and of course they flew exclusively in daylight, unlike we 'night birds.' Nevertheless, their survival rate seemed disproportionately high. It was very rare for all crew members to pull through when an aircraft of Bomber Command bit the dust, in fact records prove that the number of prisoners taken by the Germans was less than the number of 'planes shot down! Sobering, to say the least.

One of the most prevalent rumours had it that there was an unwritten agreement between the Luftwaffe and the USAF, that if a bomber dropped its undercarriage (at whatever altitude) the fighter would lay off, allowing the crew of the bomber to bale out. I would hate to think there was any truth in that particular rumour, but when recently I heard of the extraordinary number of US aircraft that defected to both Sweden and Switzerland during the war's latter years, and I still wonder if the ranks of the Caterpillar Club were swollen by impostors. (The Caterpillar Club was founded in the 20's and is exclusively for those who have been obliged to jump from an aircraft in distress. Anyone jumping for any other reason does not qualify).

Despite the lengthy inquiries, I never succeeded in contacting any other survivors of the Heilbron raid apart from George, Bill, Eric and myself. We knew that Eric, being a sergeant, would have been sent to a camp for NCOs, but it seemed inconceivable that after the atrocious flying conditions we had encountered on 4th December, that others hadn't met a similar fate. In fact, after repatriation, I re-visited Spilsby, where I learned that on that fateful night, no less than four Lancs failed to return to base (two from 207 and two from 44 [Rhodesian] Squadron, who shared Spilsby with us) and of the 28 crew members, only we four lived to tell the tale. Altogether, twelve Lancs failed to return, and I have yet to hear of anyone else who survived. Certainly, we led charmed lives, and are left with the great imponderable – why us? However, I digress –

# CHAPTER TEN

# RUSSKI HE COME

The arrival of March brought blustery but slightly warmer weather. My Canadian friend Mitch told me that the climate on the southern shores of the Baltic was uncannily like parts of Canada, with the cold dry conditions; in fact, if you ignored the menacing barbed wire and concentrated on the vista of pine clad slopes sweeping down to the water's edge, the similarity with the northern shores of Lake Superior with which he was conversant brought a lump to his throat.

Inexorably, we crossed off the days on the calendar, each seemingly longer than the last. 2nd April arrived, my 22nd birthday and to my surprise and delight, Johnnie Evans produced a cake to mark the occasion. Goodness only knows how he came by the ingredients, but from the gleam in Digger's eyes as we ate it, I have no doubt that his 'rabbit out of the hat' expertise had been involved. I seemed to have compressed more into the last year than all the preceding ones put together; all those young faces, buoyant with life and rich in potential, that had flitted momentarily across the screen of my life – sacrificed to the gods of war. When would we ever learn?

On the following day, the German guards were making one of their periodic inspections of our living quarters. After one or two jocular comments regarding the dearth of timber around the place, they turned to George's bunk. He had, by means known only to himself, succeeded in keeping several photos of his very pretty Aussie girl-friend Enid and they were pinned up on the wall, where he could see them from his bed. We all enjoyed looking at them, they were a tangible link with the real world and as far as I know, George was the only one to have pictures of his nearest and dearest, as it was against all the rules to carry personal photos or papers on Ops – they might have all sorts of incriminating complications.

However, George had somehow managed it and the sight of Enid was a great morale booster. The two guards, who like many of their ilk were bi-lingual, paused to gaze leeringly at the photos and switching from English to German in mid-sentence, made what were obviously derogatory remarks. Out of the corner of my eye I watched George, his hackles rising – you didn't have to understand German to interpret the innuendo. Then, just when he could contain himself no longer, we grabbed his arms – and for a second time solitary confinement, or worse, was averted. I was amazed, despite all our privations, at the sheer strength of the man; it took four of us to restrain him – they say love is a great motivator!

As April progressed, it became evident from reports received that we weren't going to be freed by 'us' but by 'them.' The Allies were advancing eastwards to a demarcation line at Lubeck and no further. So we had to reconcile ourselves to the fact that the Red Army was to have the privilege of removing our metaphorical shackles. Naturally, our disappointment was intense, but slowly we began to come to terms with the situation – after all, the sole object was freedom and the manner in which it was achieved of secondary importance.

News filtered through from outside the camp; the town of Barth was in turmoil and the Mayor was only one of many who had taken their own lives, rather than face the Red retribution.

It was obvious that the War was now in its dying throes and the growing tension became unbearable. Then we heard that Group Captain Weir and the senior American Officer, Colonel Zemke, had been summoned to a meeting with the German Camp Commandant, Colonel Warnstedt, who told them that he had received orders from Berlin to move all Stalag personnel westwards, en bloc, immediately! Upon receiving this ultimatum, the Allied officers, only too aware of the pitifully weak state of most of the inmates, stated categorically that to do so was out of the question. That being so, what was the German reaction? Colonel Warnstedt, who either had a spark of humanity, or a keen sense of self-preservation (methinks the latter), said that, come what may, there was to be no bloodshed and that if we refused to move, he and his staff would evacuate the place and leave us to conduct our own liberation! When the Germans left, it was up to the POWs to take over the camp peacefully and assume full control. Whatever would the Fuhrer think of that?

So it came to pass that at 1 a.m. on 30th April, the Jerries slunk silently away, leaving us to our own devices – just like that! We awoke that morning, rubbed our eyes and looked out upon a changed world, although this was not immediately apparent. Then, as the bush telegraph swung into action, a buzz of excitement pervaded Stalag Luft I and we gazed up at the hated Posten boxes in disbelief – not a coal-scuttle in sight!

The gates into the German compound stood ajar and like a tidal wave we swept in, to be confronted, unbelievably, with hut after hut full to overflowing, with Red Cross food parcels! These last four months we had existed on less than basic Jerry rations, our strength ebbing away, while the Germans had been stock-piling parcels destined for us and living like fighting cocks. If only we could lay our hands on their Teutonic throats! We hoped fervently that our late captors had run foul of the Ruskies after vacating the camp, but it was rather a forlorn hope – it was certain that no German would head east of his own volition.

There was a natural tendency to over-indulge after all our privations – the effect of too much food too soon on our undernourished stomachs could have dire consequences. So with great self discipline it was decided to share some of the parcels out, keeping the remainder in reserve.

Our overriding problem, of course, was to try and contact the Russian forces. We knew they were in the vicinity, but just how near and in what strength we had no way of knowing. Things were ominously quiet outside, not even the odd rifle shot or distant explosion to give us a clue.

So it was decided to send out a Recce patrol, bedecked with Stars and Stripes, Union Jacks, and, for good measure, a white flag of truce. A German car was commandeered and an American Major, a British Officer who spoke German and another Yank who spoke Russian sallied bravely forth, their ears ringing with Kriegie cheers.

First, they visited Barth, no Ruskies there, just rows of apathetic German civilians, mostly the very young and the very old, sitting and waiting, looking as though they expected the tumbrils to arrive at any minute to take them to the guillotine!

Next the scouts decided to proceed to the main Stralsund – Rostock road, some 15 kilometres south of the camp, to await there for any signs of Russian spearheads. The patrol returned rather despondently in the evening; still no sign of the Russian Army, but they were on their way!

The following morning the patrol ventured forth once more and this time were successful almost immediately. As they approached Barth they encountered a group of the most blood-thirsty looking scoundrels they had ever clapped eyes on; Russian guerilla fighters, equipped with a motley collection of arms and uniform, garnered during an enormous advance that stretched right back to Stalingrad. Several of them were females, but it was hard to tell he from she.

'Angliski' shouted the scouts and were immediately submerged in a sea of back-slapping odiferous bodies, with dirty, grinning Slavonic faces. They escorted our trio to a young officer who was presumably in charge. He was 1st Lt. Alec Nick Karmyzoff, an infantry regular and together the little group wended its way to our Main Gate, there to be received ecstatically by our senior officers and Stalag Luft I was officially liberated, although we were ordered to stay put, pending transportation arrangements.

At first the reality of what had happened didn't sink in. Many, especially the old sweats, seemed to be in a state of shock – the unbelievable had actually happened and now that the longed for freedom beckoned, it was somehow beyond comprehension.

Then, as if by magic, large quantities of Schnapps materialised and soon it was searing Kriegie throats and loosening their tongues. We sang all the appropriate songs from *Nellie Dean* to *Roll out the Barrel*. It didn't take long for our under-nourished constitutions to succumb to the demon alcohol and I must admit that the following few hours are something of an aberration!

Lt. Karmyzoff was soon as high as a kite. He led his band of cut-throats to the barracks housing the Russian POWs where, after a rapturous reception, he stood on a table and delivered a speech, punctuated by grins and hiccups, that had all his compatriots in stitches. My old friend Ivan Ivanovitch was very much to the fore and with beaming face he stood and proposed a toast to his liberators. The last time I saw him, he was sitting with his arm around one of the girl guerillas (at least I think, and hope, it was a girl!) singing Russian marching songs in a voice so discordant and off-key that it made your toes curl. I had always thought that all Russians, like the Welsh, could sing tunefully, but Ivan, admittedly the worse for wear, was certainly an exception to the rule.

The following day the Red Army proper arrived in the shape of a squadron of tanks. The contrast between the tank crews and the guerillas was quite remarkable. Apparently it was policy to push the guerillas ahead of the regular troops, that way they bore the brunt of any opposition encountered – they were in fact cannon fodder. The tank personnel had obviously been briefed before their arrival and came smartly turned out and to our astonishment were followed by the appearance of a brass band! That evening, in the camp theatre cum church, we sat entranced as the band, which doubled as a choir, assaulted our ear-drums for a couple of hours. There followed a communist propaganda film, with some horrendous shots of Mother Russia in the wake of the German advances earlier in the war. They certainly weren't wasting time getting to work on us; perhaps they thought that following our recent experiences, we were ripe for conversion to Stalinism.

When the initial euphoria was over, the frustration of having been liberated but still being interned began taking effect. Although we had been instructed to stay put, some of the Americans decided to do their own thing. The camp was within sight of the Baltic and nearby was a fishing village. A party of Yanks reckoned that enough was enough, promptly commandeered some boats and were last seen heading north towards Sweden. This, despite warnings from we who had sown mines in that area. Throughout the war the RAF had flown hundreds of mine-laying trips (gardening, in RAF parlance) to all the Scandinavian waters, sowing thousands of mines (vegetables) in the process. I often wonder how many of those foolhardy young men made it to Sweden.

Not to be out-done, many more of our transatlantic friends, unable to resist the urge, decided to take a chance and walk westwards towards the Allied lines. They improvised ruck-sacks, on which were sported home-made stars and stripes and, despite warnings that there were still marauding bands of Germans and Russians loose in the vicinity, off they went to meet their fate. On enquiry, it transpired that, almost to a man, these 'dissidents' were comparatively new arrivals.

The British contingent stood fast; in fact, we virtually took over the running of the camp, striving to bring at least some semblance of order into what was potentially an explosive situation.

Following the raid on the local Bols distillery in Barth, a group of Yanks, very much the worse for wear, thought it a good idea to set fire to the Posten boxes, one of which crashed ablaze onto a barrack block, which fortunately was empty at the time. Only prompt action from hundreds of more sober Kriegies, who formed a chain of buckets from the nearest water hydrant, prevented the fire from spreading and causing far more devastation.

Our Russian liberators, in a rather over-the-top bizarre gesture, plundered the local farms and drove live-stock into the camp, specifically for our delectation. There being a chronic lack of butchers among us, the ex POWs were obliged to improvise and the sports field soon resembled a battlefield, as beasts were crudely slaughtered, bonfires lit and soon the air was filled with the mouth-watering aroma of pork chops and lamb cutlets being grilled. The end products were tough, black and smoky, but it was certainly the only fresh meat any of us had tasted since incarceration.

Day followed endless day and always the answer to our pathetic pleading was the same: "Sit tight, it won't be long."' Some of our chaps with a literary bent managed to infiltrate the offices of the local press (German journalism was, for once, lost for words) and succeeded in producing a souvenir news sheet, a two page production aptly named *Barth Hard Times,* which relates to the events leading up to and the liberation of, Stalag Luft I. I still have my copy, now yellowed and tatty, but its contents have proved invaluable as a mind jogger. Its reporting is concise and undramatic, but this is not unexpected, as the reporters themselves were men used to terse jargon of service dispatches and not given to hyperbole. Its date of publication was Saturday, 5th May, 1945; we had been 'free' then for five days. Avidly we listened to the BBC news bulletin and when VE Day was announced on 8th May, the temptation to run 'amok' became almost irresistible, especially when we heard of the celebrations back in England and practically everywhere else in the so-called civilised world.

During my stay as a guest of the German Government, I had received no mail and had no idea if any of the letters I had written had ever left Germany – perhaps, like the Red Cross parcels, they had failed to reach their destination. Never much of a telepath, I nevertheless 'knew' that the folks back home were thinking of me, just as I was of them. I had no idea, of course, if they had been informed of my survival.

We celebrated as best we could; Johnnie Evans made a super Kriegie cake from the contents of the now available food parcels and we washed it down with illicitly procured Bols. Surely now that hostilities were officially at an end, the powers that be would pull the necessary strings and release us from this friendly Russian strangle-hold.

The announcement of VE Day triggered off yet more American 'defections' and there were ominous rumblings from our own compound. The one gratifying aspect of the whole frustrating affair was that we were able to feed our undernourished bodies and to feel the strength returning to erstwhile wobbly limbs. Our shrunken frames responded dramatically as the calorie input soared and the improvement wasn't only physical. Suddenly, the pent-up uncertainties of the last harrowing months were dissipated, as the light at the end of the tunnel grew ever brighter.

The weather was fabulous, with the sun pleasantly warm and the skies cloudless. The place resembled a very disheveled holiday camp, as grateful Kriegies discarded their various assortment of clothing and lounged in the sunshine. It was as if we had two quite separate entities; our mmds and thoughts were already back home with our loved ones, while physically we strove to come to terms with a situation over which we had no jurisdiction.

Our Russian hosts were not to blame for the unwarranted delay, and although Red Army uniform was a vast improvement on field grey, we began to think of them as custodians, which albeit unwittingly, they were.

# BARTH

# HARD TIMES

Vol 1   No. 1   LAST 1   SATURDAY MAY 5th 1945   PRICE 1 D- BAR.

Editor: F|L E. R. INKPEN   Assoc: 1st Lt N. GIDDINGS   Publisher: 1st Lt D. MacDONALD   Printing: F|LT J. D. WHITE

# RUSSKY COME!

As seen by LOWELL BENNET. I. N. S. War Correspondent.

WHAT D'YE KNOW- JOE!!

## RELIEVED!

Colonel Zemke intended to write this appreciation of the relief of Stalag Luft I, but unfortunately necessary duties have made this impossible. He has, in his own words, "taken a powder" to make final arrangements with the relieving Soviet forces.

It is therefore my privilege to introduce this Memorial Edition of the BARTH HARD TIMES. During the successes, reverse and stagnant periods encountered during this struggle, our newspaper has faithfully recorded the German war communiques and expanded upon them in capable editorials.

With the redemption of a continent, our exile is ended. Our barbbound community will soon be a memory. So, on behalf of Colonel Hubert Zemke and myself, to all our fellow-kriegies: G O O D LUCK!

G./C. C. T. Weir.

## BRAITHWAITE FINDS UNCLE JOE

### Contacts Russian Infantryman at Crossroads
### Five miles South of Stalag One.

Major Braithwaite and Sgt Korson, our Stalag scouts, raced out to a cross-roads 5 miles south of Barth with the order, "find Uncle Joe". This was 8 p. m., May 1.

They searched southward, defying a rumored Russian curfew which was about as brief and emphatic as their own order: "EVERYONE stay put; anyone seen moving will be shot on sight."

Meanwhile, Wing Commander Blackburn's telephone crew were ringing numbers in Stralsund, hoping a Russian would answer the phone and we could break the big news of our presence. "Try the mayor," they asked the girl (who was still working Barth's phone exchange). "Not a chance," said she. "Barth's mayor poisoned himself and Stralsund's mayor has sprouted wings."

Scouts Braithwaite and Korson pushed on 3 miles. The scenery: thousands of people everywhere, sitting down, waiting.

# LIFE AND DEATH OF A GERMAN TOWN

### TENSE MOMENTS WHILE ALLIES TAKE CONTROL

An air of tension hung over the camp for many days. The presence of the English and American armies on the Elbe and the Russian encirclement of Berlin made everyone feel that the end must be near. The commencement of a new Russian drive across the lower Oder toward the Baltic ports finally increased the tension to an almost unbearable pitch. Panic reigned in the Vorlager. No German had any more interest in guarding the prisoners, but only in saving his own life. Confidential reports were hurriedly burnt — and copies of "Mein Kampf" went to swell the flames.

#### Conference with the Kommandant

Finally, late in the afternoon, the Senior British and American officers were called to a conference with the German camp Kommandant Colonel Warnstedt. They were told that orders had been received to move the whole camp westward. Colonel Zemke stated he was not willing to move at all, and asked in that case what the German attitude would be. The Commandant replied that he would not tolerate bloodshed in the camp; if we did not intend to move, he and his men would evacuate themselves and leave us in sole possession of the camp. When the Germans left it would be up to us to take over the camp peacefully and assume full control.

At approximately 1 A.M. on April 30 Major Steinhauer informed Group Captain Weir and Colonel Zemke that the Germans had evacuated the camp, leaving it in our charge. When the camp woke up in the morning it was to find itself no longer under armed guard and comparatively free.

#### Where are the Russians?

Our next problem was to establish contact with the Russian forces. It was decided to send out something in the nature of a recco patrol. An American Major, a British Officer speaking German, and an American Officer speaking Russian, set out with the German in the auto which was equipped with an American flag on one fender and a white flag on the other, to investigate the real situation in Barth and then proceed to the main Stralsund – Rostock road, some 15 kilometers south of the camp, to wait there for any signs of Russian spearheads or of the proximity of the front line. The first patrol returned in the early evening. Still no sign or news of the Russian Army, but they were coming!

**Russian Contact (con. from Page 1)** Every house draped with red flags (who said the Germans weren't chameleons?). Suddenly, there was Uncle Joe — — or one of his ambassadors: a chunky little Dead End guy who loomed up and flashed a variety of lethal weapons and a cacophony of Slavic language.

"Engliski", shouted the scouts.
"Never mind the words", said Joe's man, "this isn't Dulag" or something like that in Russian. And, without ceremony they went to the nearest Russian officer. It was 1st Lt. Alec Nick Karmyzoff, infantryman from Tula (you oughta see that written in Russian!) He'd fought his way from Stalingrad — three years across Russia, Poland and Germany — to the relief of Stalag Luft I.

**Toasts are Drunk.**

Karmyzoff came in the main gate. Commanding Officers Zemke and Weir received him. Schnapps seared kriegie throats — glasses smashed Hitler's picture, the barracks jiggled with cheering and back-pounding. Toasts were drunk: "To the destruction of Germany — she will never rise again! And to our solid and enduring friendship." Karmyzoff went to the Russian barracks (our co-kriegies) — told them about himself, their army and the new life that was beginning. Thus the first contact. Karmyzoff bedded down on the floor — "Rather the floor than a German bed," said he. BBC announced Hitler dead; kriegies heard the "Hit Parade" from home; the excitement was exhausting. — But what an experience!

### QUAKING BARTH BURGHERS BOW BEFORE REDS

As Russian tanks rumbled Northwards on the cobblestone roads from Stralsund, as Russian cavalry and guerilla troops tore hell bent for the Baltic, as the spluttering German radio flashed a staccato of place names that had gone under in the Red rip tide, Barth became an open city and an open grave. The few Americans who had been in town on camp chores from Stalag I knew that the life of Barth was a living death. We had seen the streets peopled by children and octogenerians, we had noticed that all males were either lame, halt, or blind; we had stared into empty shop windows, and we had seen the soldiers of the master race straggle back from the fronts dazed, whipped, harbingers of the ruin that stalked the streets of German towns. By April 30, this year of grace, the good burghers of Barth turned their faces to the wall and stopped hoping.

#### LET 'EM EAT CAKE

Life had not been good. In the bakery shop where the camp brot was made hung a sign; cake is not sold to Jews or Poles. It failed to explain that cake was not sold to the supermen either. There was no cake. But there were good things to eat in the larders of Barth,baking powder requisitioned from Holland, Nestles milk commandee...d from Denmark, wines looted from the cellars of France, spaghetti and noodles hijacked from Italy, Worcestershire sauce which had trickled through mysteriously from England, olive oil drained from Greece, in short, all types of blood from the turnip of Europe. If Mussolini considered the Mediterranean his sea, Hitler considered the world his oyster and was trying to serve it up to the Reich on the half shell.

#### A House of Cards

As the first explosions from the flak school reverberated under the sullen Baltic sky, the new order toppled on Barth like a house of cards. Red flags and white sheets began to appear in the windows of the ginger bread houses. Flight was futile and the old stood querously on their door steps, wringing gnarled hands and weeping. Pictures of Hitler were torn down and scattered like confetti. Two German children came wailing into the bakery shop. They had heard American airmen ate little boys and mother said the day of reckoning was at hand.

Barth, like the whole of Deutschland-über-alles Germany, was on its knees in terror. But mayhem did not materialize. Wine, not blood, flowed through the streets. We got drunk.

## CHAPTER ELEVEN

# AT LAST, HOME – BY THE BACK DOOR

A week after our first encounter with Uncle Joe's array of thuggery, we were briefed to try and smarten ourselves up, as Marshal Voroshiloff, a very big wig in the army hierarchy, was visiting Barth and we were to parade before him, just to show how smart and efficient we were. Air Crew, particularly those of Bomber Command, weren't exactly famous for spit and polish. Operational squadrons had their priorities right and providing the lads performed their various functions efficiently, flying personnel were left much to their own devices with regard to dress and of course, the tight schedule of flying precluded the horrors of square-bashing. Many a seasoned veteran volunteered for a second tour in order to exchange the comparatively rigorous discipline of Training Command for the more relaxed atmosphere and camaraderie of the front line squadrons.

Notwithstanding our natural aversion, we thought we'd give it a go, even though at best we looked a rag-tag bunch. One or two of the POWs, in the main RAF regulars, managed somehow to keep up appearances, maintaining that a tidy exterior helped to develop an orderly mind, but we irregular slovens had other ideas and went our own slothful way.

I remember particularly an Army paratroop major who had been captured at Arnhem and was the only 'brown job' in our compound. How he came to be in a camp for Air Force only I never knew, but he was a soldier of the old school, one of whom Kitchener would have been proud. You could see your face in his boots and cut your fingers on his trouser creases. I felt sorry for him when we had a march-past rehearsal, as he vainly strove to inculcate some semblance of co-ordination into our serried ranks.

The following morning, the sports field having been given a wash and brush-up following the preceding carnage, we were duly paraded. The Red Army band played a sort of discordant fanfare and onto the parade ground clanked the Marshal, surrounded by his acolytes. I use the word 'clanked' as it comes nearest to describing faithfully his distinctly audible progression. I had seen dignitaries and Royal personages bedecked with medals, orders and what have you, but this man was ridiculous! No mere ribbons for him, but the whole cocktail cabinet which covered his chest from shoulder to waist – both sides! He wore a sword of gargantuan proportions, the scabbard of which cut a dusty trail through the sand.

He and his entourage stood stiffly to the salute as we marched past, giving them the 'eyes right' and trying desperately to 'put some swank in it,' as our galloping Major had requested; it was like a scene from toy-town. The British contingent was in the van and as we swung away, I looked back and watched the much larger

74

American detachment as they shuffled past His Nibs. At least we had made a modicum of effort to give the occasion a shred of dignity, but they, with their mixture of crew-cuts and beards, unkempt appearance and shambling gait, gave the event an atmosphere of farce; the name Fred Karno sprang aptly to mind. However, the occasion passed off peacefully enough and I just hoped that Allied/Russian relations hadn't been irretrievably impaired. How I would have loved to have had a film of this momentous event; it would have won the award for comedy-of-the-year, even without a commentary.

Another week dragged agonisingly by. Someone started a rumour that the Ruskies weren't going to allow our people to fly in and fetch us, until all Russian ex-POWs were safely back home. I never thought I would ever feel compassion for the Germans, but already the communist screws were being tightened; Barth was like a ghost town and farms were being denuded of livestock. I know the Reds considered it to be retribution for the awful atrocities inflicted by the Wehrmacht a few years earlier, but two wrongs never did make a right. This ghastly tit-for-tat was never going to bring about that which was the objective of all the grief and sacrifice – a world at peace with itself.

In order to kill a little time, the Yanks challenged us to, of all things, a baseball match. It seemed a bit under the belt to invite us to play them at their great national game. We did, however, have some worthys who at least knew the basics – there were quite a few Canadians present and many of our chaps had trained in Canada. So, tongue in cheek, we took up the gauntlet.

The sports area was packed to overflowing and there was quite a carnival atmosphere, largely brought about by the use of cheer-leaders, who waved star spangled banners aloft and sought to lift the American contingent into a patriotic frenzy. But all their strivings were in vain, our trans-atlantic cousins, incredibly, were well and truly thrashed – it was like an 100-1 outsider winning the Derby. I have never seen a baseball game since – I figured it was best to quit while you're on top!

I'm afraid that our western allies have been taking quite a verbal battering, so I would like to redress the balance a little. I found many Americans very convivial and enjoyed their company immensely. But it was when these self-same men, who were charming as individuals, became motivated en masse that the rot seemed to set in. I was reminded strongly of the lynch-mobs so often seen in the Hollywood Westerns, where a rabble rouser incites a crowd of normally docile citizens to dispense rough justice. Suffice it to say that, during those interminable three weeks, when the British closed ranks and held firm, like Wellington's squares at Waterloo, I felt a sudden surge of patriotism which surprised me, as I had never been a member of the flag-wagging brigade.

Just when despair really began to gnaw at our vitals and we were on the verge of breaking ranks, we received telephone confirmation that B-17s (Flying Fortresses) of the US Eighth Air Force were being dispatched from England, to start a re-patriation lift from a nearby aerodrome that had been a base for Junkers 88 fighter/bombers. Uncle Joe had at long last relented.

Suddenly the long wait was over and we were marched to the airfield. (This was really travelling light; there were no luggage problems!). Prior to leaving the Stalag,

75

we were told that we might have to wait for some hours before the aircraft arrived and that, should they not do so, we would have to return to camp until the following day. Also, there were many German 'planes littering the airfield, but we were to give them a wide berth, in case of 'booby traps'. But for some the lure of souvenirs was too great and as we lounged around, waiting for our messiahs to arrive, there was the sharp crack of an explosion and Brooklyn was minus a son. What a stupid, wholly unnecessary waste of a life!

Then, as we stood looking aghast at the smoking remains of a Ju88, in the distance, growing louder by the second came the rumble of a multitude of aero-engines, until the air reverberated with the glorious song of liberation. Some wiseacre piped up: "Fancy sending Fort's, they should have sent Liberators!" (the Liberator was the other, lesser known, four-engined day bomber operated by the USAF). Then the sky was full of B-17s and we stood there cheering our heads off as one by one the menacing, but to our eyes oh so beautiful aircraft peeled off and nosed in to land.

Strange, but when we first learned we were to be air-lifted out, it was automatically assumed that our own Queen of the Skies, the Lancaster, would be our instrument of deliverance. This really was very presumptuous of us, with the preponderance of Yanks in the Stalag.

As we clambered gratefully aboard, the expected buzz of excitement was conspicuous by its absence; each man seemed to retire into his shell, to his own private world. Perhaps we were all thinking of the last time we left Mother Earth; lady luck had smiled on each and every one of us and we had survived against enormous odds. Our numbers, compared to those who would never return, were so pitifully small.

Next to me on the improvised seating was Paul Johnson, who had baled out of a Fairey Battle way back in 1940. When taken prisoner, he had held the rank of Pilot Officer and of course POWs don't get promotions! He had previously related to me how, late in 1944, a much decorated Wing Commander had arrived at Barth. When Paul had been shot down, this worthy had been a Corporal Air Gunner! This ironic situation was not an isolated one; there were many similar instances. Life can be very fickle.

The big bomber taxied around the perimeter track, paused facing into the runway, then the engines bellowed and she surged forward. As soon as we were airborne, the pilot turned sharply to starboard and flew low over the Stalag. Looking down we could see the camp from an unaccustomed angle, with its neat rows of deserted huts going seemingly on and on. Along the road stretched a long crocodile of humanity, wending its sinuous way towards the airfield and freedom. I wondered absently what had become of our Group Captain's horse. The Russians had presented him with a beautiful stallion, donated involuntarily by some German horse-breeder and everyone was wondering how he was going to get it back to England – there certainly wasn't room in a Flying Fort. I never did get to know the outcome of this curious affair, so if anyone knows . . . The trip back to England was made at low altitude, as we had no oxygen and the B-17 was, of course, unpressurised. So we had a Cooks Tour of Northern Germany, with its spectral towns and also Holland and Belgium. We passed near Waicheren, where about a hundred years ago we had bombed the sea walls and poor old Jock had collected his chunk of shrapnel. The scene was still one of watery devastation and one's heart went out to those poor innocents whose homes and lands had been despoiled. Doubtless the powers that be had been justified in ordering the dykes to be breached and probably many Allied lives had been saved, but it was an awful price to pay and left the Dutch with a daunting task of reclamation.

Then, after a short hop across the North Sea, we were heading up the English Channel, with everyone jostling for a vantage point, we all wanted to view those famous white Cliffs, then perhaps we could really convince ourselves it wasn't all just a dream. I finished up wedged in the starboard 'midships gun position, along with several others and we watched enthralled as the land of our birth (or adoption) hove into view; that unforgettable vista that symbolised a free world and for centuries had taunted so many would-be predators. I must admit that many a normally stiff upper lip trembled – mine amongst them.

We headed in over the coast and gazed longingly down at the once so-familiar patch-work quilt of fields, with their aura of utter peace. Finally as we touched down at Poole in Dorset, I looked at the faces of those around me. There was George, almost unrecognisable from the skeletal figure of only a few weeks ago, looking bronzed and fit, with only one thought in mind – to get back to Aussie and his Enid as soon as was humanly possible. Bill seemed as enigmatic as ever, but the haunted look had gone from his eyes and his face lit up at the prospect of returning to Wagga and being re-united with his family. Ron Winton's face had made a remarkable recovery, the Baltic sunshine had worked wonders and only the schnozz bore evidence of his own private bit of the war. Digger Hassall, his trading days over, sat looking rather smug with his pocketful of IOUs – if things went to plan, he would shortly be joining the ranks of the world's plutocrats, but you know what they say about birds in the hand and at that precise moment we hadn't a bean between us.

Alex Delage, puffing away at his trusty briar, for once seemed lost for words. No doubt his mind was somewhere in his beloved Poland; I know he was worried to distraction about his kin there and was wondering if and when he would be permitted entry into the land of his birth. His contact with the Russians at Barth had done nothing to allay his fears.

And so it was that we crept back into Old England by the back door, as it were. The War had been officially over for a little more than a fortnight and the initial jubilation had subsided. As we trod the hallowed ground of home once more, some of our number, in very un-RAF-like manner, knelt to kiss, à la Pope John Paul, the Holy Grail.

Our minds were in turmoil. To be back at last was indeed wonderful, but we knew only too well what the price of 'victory' had been and our hearts went out to the countless families, all over the world, who were grieving the loss of someone near and dear, even amid the celebrations. To my mind the Air Crew of Bomber Command were an elite. Fighter pilots did fantastic deeds of derring do, but to sit tight on a seemingly endless bombing run, with flak flying and night fighters on the prowl, required a very special and different kind of courage. I felt a surge of pride at having been associated with this modest, self-effacing race of supermen. I doubt we shall ever see their like again.

# CHAPTER TWELVE

# A LAND FIT FOR HEROES?

At this time of high emotion, the RAF reception machinery swung smoothly into action and we were whisked off to a large marquee where, without preamble we were invited to partake of a meal that I still rate as the best I've ever tasted. It consisted merely of home-made bread, farmhouse butter, strawberry jam and, best of all, steaming hot mugs of tea – nectar of the gods!

No sooner had we gorged ourselves on the oh so typically English fare, than we were shepherded onto a specially chartered train. On reflection, I suspect the prime reason for this was to keep us segregated from the population at large. Although we had performed our ablutions before leaving Barth, we still looked a bedraggled bunch of ruffians, certainly in no fit state to be turned loose on an unsuspecting public.

The train, so utterly different from those previously encountered on the European Grand Tour, chugged merrily through countryside alive with the magic of Spring – we had returned just in time to see rural England at its incomparable best. There was a marked absence of badinage, so engrossed were we all with our private thoughts. Since leaving the Stalag, it was almost as if we were cocooned, after all the endless hours we had spent debating and planning for the future. I remembered so many conversations, most of which started with – "If we ever get out of this place alive, I'm going to . . ." – there followed a veritable catalogue of all the do-goodery with which we were going to re-shape Western civilisation, and our own bit of it in particular.

After what seemed no time at all, we were jolted out of our reveries by the train slowing to a halt at Cosford railway station. Cosford is one of those rather unique establishments that boasts its very own station and right across its portals were emblazoned in huge letters – 'WELCOME HOME'. Our Alma Mater was rolling out the metaphorical red carpet, welcoming us back to her bosom. It's a very pleasant feeling to know you are not forgotten and that despite all the victory celebrations, someone quite high in the hierarchy had had the forethought to display those two significant words. We might not be heroes, but were not entirely unsung.

The RAF machine swung yet again into action with formidable efficiency and within no time we were subjected to an obviously well rehearsed routine, with de-lousing and bathing, followed by the inevitable service haircut. Then our entire wardrobe was committed to the furnace and we were kitted out from head to toe with new apparel, complete with rank and insignia. Photos were taken, new identity cards issued and of course, travel warrants. Having completed all these very necessary preliminaries, they bundled us off to bed like naughty schoolboys. We needed no rocking, it had been quite a day and in the morning they were going to turn us all loose, to go our separate ways and hopefully realise some of the many dreams and aspirations so often voiced these long last months and years. The very fact that there really was a future and that perhaps some of those dreams could become reality, was something our bewildered minds were very slow to grasp.

So the following morning, spick and span in our squeaky new Battle Dress, we breakfasted early and after exchanging addresses and promising faithfully to keep in touch (at the time we really meant it!), we commenced the homeward lap of our ultimate operation. My orders were to go home and await instructions, a situation I was very happy to comply with.

I entrained to London, crossing by underground to Waterloo, where my mind went back to the last leave before the Heilbronn fiasco. My arrival had coincided with an air-raid warning and I had dutifully followed the crowd down into what for many of them was a second home – the Underground. It was at the time of the V1 (Doodlebug) assault upon London and the south-east. As a result of the alert, all outgoing trains were cancelled and I settled down to a night of very little sleep, but an abundance of cockney humour. How they managed to keep up the cheerful patter after so many years of living like troglodytes was beyond me and when just after dawn the 'all clear' sounded, I made my rather befuddled way back up to the real world, it was with a greatly revised opinion of the civilian population of London – I would far rather take my chances up in the limitless sky than in their claustrophobic world. In the early hours of the morning a doodle-bug had scored a near miss on the station, making our teeth rattle, but the little group of buskers down below, giving out with their very own rendition of *Roll out the Barrel* never missed a beat.

But now that was all ancient history and I was leaving a battered but unbowed London and heading back to my roots, seeing the familiar countryside with new eyes. I had sent a telegram to my folks from Cosford, warning them of my pending arrival, but not stating any specific time; I would much rather just arrive, preferably through the back door. This was just as well, as I missed the last train home from Waterloo and was obliged to spend yet another, but much more comfortable night in London. As a result, I entrained at 6 a.m. and the air of expectancy grew as we huffed and puffed our way along the old familiar route – Woking-Brookwood-Farnborough – and at long last FLEET! What marvellous timing – just in time for breakfast!

I savoured the mile-long walk from the station to my home, drinking in the well-remembered scenes, with their boyhood associations, so indelibly stamped on my mind.

On arrival, I paused at the gate, taking in with one sweeping glance the neatly trimmed hedges, the garden a profusion of flowers and the warm red brickwork of the Victorian cottage that was my ancestral home. How often had I visualised it during those long months of separation and I hesitated before entering the family domain, struggling to control my emotions. After all, I was supposed to be a battle-hardened veteran, not a wet-eyed wimp!

Tip-toeing up the path, I peered in at the kitchen window and there, oblivious of me, was a figure, topped by hair a little whiter than I last remembered, bustling industriously about her domestic chores; a light tap on the glass and a face turned towards me, the expression changing instantly from inquiry to delight and joy. I let out a whoop, which brought Dad running from the direction of the chicken-house; I had obviously caught them on the hop, but that only made homecoming more enjoyable.

Mum and Dad told me of the agony of not knowing that they had been obliged to endure. They'd had a telegram from the squadron on the day following the Heilbronn raid, when I was posted missing. Then nothing until 16th January, 1945, when they received another telegram telling them that my name had been mentioned in a German broadcast as being a POW, but they were to treat the information with reserve pending confirmation, which followed soon after. No wonder Mum's hair was shades whiter – all those weeks, including Christmas, hoping for the best and fearing the worst.

The next few days were largely spent renewing old acquaintances and catching up on the back-log of news, both local and national. I was deeply distressed to hear that during my incarceration, Phil, one of the original Fleet quartet, had been killed shortly before hostilities ceased. They had been on a raid to Nuremburg and the Halifax had gone down with all hands. Fleet itself was still its rather old-fashioned dozy self; the frenzied commuter boom that erupted in the '50s and '60s was still only a gleam in the property developers' eyes.

And so, after four years, during which my life, in line with countless others, had changed beyond all recognition, I could at last turn my sights to the future with something like confidence.

But first and foremost I must return to the scene of the crime – Spilsby. A 'phone call confirmed that 207 were still in residence and so I made my nostalgic pilgrimage to find an airfield peopled by strangers. Stupidly, I had forgotten all about the pathetic survival rate of blokes in our line of business. Looking frustratedly around for familiar faces, at last I saw one; it was Joyce Brotherton, a white-haired Waaf Admin. Officer, a sort of matriarchal figure who was always to be seen standing at the caravan whenever we took off, her head hatless and the hair shining like a beacon among the little row of faithfuls gathered to wave us on our way.

I was flattered that she recognised me on sight – she had seen so very many come and go. Meeting her made the whole trip worthwhile, even though she confirmed the grim news that on the fateful night of 4th December, 207 had lost two Lancs, as also had 44 squadron and that from the four aircraft, we four alone had survived. How lucky can you get? So, in chastened mood, I beat a retreat, wondering at my good fortune. Four out of 28; what right had I to be here in the land of the living, surrounded by Mother Nature in all her glory? My mind flew back to the bale-out, reliving the feeling of abject terror that gripped me as I hacked frenziedly at the rear-door of our Lanc; it was so very nearly 3 out of 28. There but for the grace of God . . .

Before departing from Spilsby, I popped into The Bell, which thankfully was just the same, albeit peopled by ghosts. Mine host was as affable as ever, but became rather confused when I started to inquire after the health or otherwise of my contemporary aviators. He said so many airmen had crossed the portals of The Bell during the last couple of years that they seemed to blur into a sort of universal image dressed in blue. Strangely, he did remember Joe and asked after his welfare. I found this most surprising, as if anyone ever qualified for the title anonymous, it was him. I was able to tell the landlord that according to Joyce Brotherton, Joe and his mates had beaten 'The Reaper' and survived the tour, after a whole series of 'dicey' Ops, but then, how could it have been otherwise!

As I left Spilsby, there was every sign that its days as a Bomber Command airfield would shortly be over and that the brash, ear-splitting roar of Merlins would soon be replaced by the gentle put-put of diesel tractors. Life in rural Lincolnshire would resume its placid rhythm and in the centuries to come the locals would talk reminiscently of those far distant days in the 20th Century, when their native heath was tenanted by a breed of men whose deeds, performed so unpretentiously, put those of King Arthur and his knights to shame.

Following repatriation, I had applied to undergo a course in Photography, that being my civilian trade. To my delight I was instructed to report to No.1 School of Photography, which just happened to be at Farnborough, only 4 miles from my home at Fleet! So I had the great advantage of 'living out' at home. The course was one for Photographic Officers, and I found it absorbing. On completion, it was with intense satisfaction that I was retained at the school as officer in charge of airmans training, with the rank of Flight Lieutenant; so I continued to enjoy the benefits of home cooking.

However, disenchantment with life in the RAF soon followed. Most of the chaps undergoing training were ex-operational NCOs feverishly awaiting their demob. Heaven only knows why they were sent on a course in photography at this juncture, when their over-riding ambition was to throw off their service shackles and become just plain 'Misters' again. Despite frantic efforts by the Air Force hierarchy, all attempts to enforce discipline failed miserably and the situation became almost chaotic. I found myself caught between two stools, feeling sympathy for the chaps in their dilemma, yet having to side with authority in trying to attain some semblance of law and order. Nothing could be further removed from the wonderful camaraderie experienced on the operational squadrons during the recent hostilities and I felt a great sadness at the turn of events.

Somehow the storm was weathered and the violence that at one time seemed inevitable never materialised, averted perhaps by the knowledge that for most of them, freedom was just around the corner.

For some time I had been pondering my future; whether to try and pursue my new found job as an RAF Photographer, or to try my luck in the free-for-all of civvy street. A friend and former colleague at work thought we should try a joint private venture and with my current disillusionment with life in the Air Force, I readily agreed.

So on 11th September, 1946, after $5^1/2$ unforgettable years, I went through the process of civilianisation, swapping one uniform for what was virtually another – the grey pin-stripe demob suit. The great adventure was over and, unlike so many others, fortune, lady luck, fate, or perhaps a little of each had smiled upon me. The future, which so often had seemed non-existent, now beckoned and eagerly I moved forward, ready to meet the challenge of life in the brave new world which we were told was about to emerge from the seemingly unending years of strife.

# CHAPTER THIRTEEN

# PATRICK AND JOSEPH
# UNRAVEL THE PB765 MYSTERY

In a little village with the Germanic sounding name of Holtzwihr, near to the beautiful old town of Colmar in Alsace, France, the date of 27th January holds great significance. On that day in 1945, after five years of suffering and subservience, the occupying German forces were finally driven westwards back into their Fatherland, leaving Holtzwihr little more than a shattered shell, with over 90% of its picturesque buildings destroyed.

Little wonder then, that every year at this time the liberation of the area is celebrated by the whole community, who gather to give thanks and to remember their less fortunate compatriots who perished in the battles that raged in and around their village in the weeks prior to its liberation.

The celebrations of January 1985 were even more special than those of preceding years, being the 40th anniversary of the great day. In addition to the service of remembrance at the strikingly modern looking church which had replaced the more traditional one destroyed in January 1945, there had been a feast laid on in the nearby village hall and, Alsace being renowned for its wines, there was no shortage of the famous local vintages.

As the afternoon wore on, the local inhabitants, replete with food and having imbibed sufficient vin to set the tongues a-wagging, fell, as was their wont on such occasions, to reminiscing. Naturally, the village elders, who could vividly recall the liberation, were regaling the young bloods with tales (often suitably embellished) of the historic and momentous happenings of the winter of 1944/45, when little Holtzwihr, which had already endured the rigours of occupation for almost five years, suddenly became a fiery inferno, as the occupying German troops opened fire on units of the American Army, entrenched in the Vosges Mountains which dominate the fertile Alsatian plain on which the village is situated. Fortunately, most of the villagers were accommodated in large air-raid shelters, but one of them received a direct hit and all the occupants, including several members of the occupying forces, died instantly.

Within days, advancing columns of American tanks fought a running battle with those of the Wehrmacht all around the area and when they finally rumbled westwards, the devastation defied description.

Among those attending the festivities were two patriotic sons of France, Patrick Baumann, a large, affable young man of about 30, employed at the local winery and Joseph Barthelemy, small, dapper and 40-ish, a bookbinder, engaged in the exacting task of restoring priceless medieval tomes in nearby Colmar's historic library.

They listened spellbound as survivors of those heady, horrendous days told of hardships endured under Nazi occupation and Patrick, who for several years had been interested in the aircraft of W.W.II (in fact he'd made an impressive range of models), pricked up his ears when two elderly sisters told the story of when, just before the battles that were to devastate their village, a large aeroplane, blazing like a meteor, had narrowly missed Holtzwihr and crashed into the nearby forest. No-one seemed to have any specific details of the incident and so Patrick, curiosity aroused, decided to explore the wooded area in question, to try and find out the whys and wherefores of this mysterious plane. What nationality was it? Were there any survivors and if so, were any still alive after more than 40 years and where on the planet were they?

He had been given an approximate location of the crash, which narrowed the field a little. After much diligent searching, deep in the undergrowth he discovered a slight indentation in the forest floor and then a small twisted piece of duralumin. Greatly encouraged, he commenced a thorough search of the area, unearthing many pieces of metal, perspex and rubber, and even oxygen bottles. One of the most interesting discoveries was an unidentifiable instrument on which the initials A.M. (Air Ministry) were clearly inscribed, so Patrick knew that this aircraft had indeed been British, dispelling village rumours that the plane had been of American origin.

Next he was faced with the dilemma of how to go about identifying the wreck. He had been told that the incident occurred on the evening of 4th December, 1944, so that was a starting point.

So began an intensive investigation that would have done credit to Sherlock Holmes himself. With Patrick supplying the drive and Joseph with his patient probing, they wrote to every conceivable source of information in both France and England. Little by little the jig-saw fitted together. They discovered that 'their' aeroplane (they felt very personally involved) was indeed a British Lancaster, namely PB 765, of 207 Squadron, RAF, which had been shot down following a raid on Heilbronn in the Ruhr. (It was in fact the only raid of any appreciable size that this particular town suffered during the entire War).

With regard to the crew, it was discovered that subsequent to the crash, the bodies of two gunners had been removed from the wreckage. These had been interred in the village churchyard, following a brief service conducted by the solitary local priest, as the villagers were forbidden to attend by the occupying Germans. After the war, the bodies were removed to the military cemetery at Choloy.

The full names and ranks of the crew were obtained from one of their many contacts, the British Ministry of Defence, but the task of discovering if in fact any of them still survived seemed at one time to be insuperable; every avenue of investigation seemed to lead to a brick wall.

By early 1988, the two friends, after three years of endeavour, were on the verge of calling it a day. In one last despairing effort, they entered an item in the British ex-servicemens' magazine *Air Mail*. It ran thus: "Inhabitants of Holtzwihr would like to get in touch with members or friends of crew of Lanc. PB 765 of 207 Sqdn based Spilsby which crashed 4/5.12.44. please write; P. Baumann, 5 Rue du Colonel Cade, Holtzwihr, 68320 Muntzenheim, France."

Having played their final card, Patrick and Joseph waited, with little hope and no confidence, hoping against hope that this last despairing cast of the net would catch a fish.

This is where fate stepped in, in the shape of my old friend and fellow Kriegie Ron Winton. It appears he was (and is) membership secretary of 207 Squadron Association (the squadron having been disbanded in the early '80s) being involved with ex-RAF personnel and those of 207 in particular, it is perhaps not surprising that he would be au fait with periodicals such as *Air Mail,* which provide invaluable information for former service comrades trying to contact old acquaintances.

So Ron (we had met just once since repatriation and that was in 1945) wrote to Patrick post haste, explaining how he, I, George and Bill had been together both on the squadron and in prison-camp. He also sent letters to George and I at our 1945 addresses, which we had exchanged at the Stalag.

Now the long arm of co-incidence lengthens. My family had long since ceased living in our former 'ancestral home' in Fleet, in fact, many years ago the old place was desecrated by builders, who converted it into flats. My sole remaining relative in the district was a dear elderly lady, a cousin of my Dad's whom we used to refer to as 'cousin Muriel'; we had not met since the War. Someone of compassion (I never knew who) forwarded Ron's letter to Muriel, who had no idea where I lived, or indeed if I lived! However, she did have the address of my brother-in-law, Dave Scott, husband of my late younger sister. Dave, who now resides in Pevensey Bay in Sussex was surprised to receive a letter from Muriel, who apologised for not phoning, as she was hard of hearing.

And so it was with great surprise that, in August of 1988, I received a phone call from Dave, with the staggering news that a young Frenchman in Alsace had done a spot of excavating and a lot of research, culminating in the identification of wreckage as being undisputably bits of our beleaguered Lanc and would I get in touch with him. Would I ever!

Suddenly, the past, for so long buried and pushed into the background of my mind by the pressure and turmoil of life in the late 20th century, arose to confront me and I was propelled back about 43 years in time, unlocking the door to times and events that had lain dormant for longer than I cared to remember.

Simultaneously, Ron's letter to George in Australia bore fruit. Again, he wrote to George at his only known address, at Victoria Park, W.A. I had kept in touch with him for several years after the War, so I knew he had indeed married his great love, Enid and that they had three children. But then, unaccountably, our correspondence had lapsed and although after a break of several years I tried to contact him, it was to no avail.

Ron, however, had better luck, and the letter he wrote found its devious way to George's present home in Attadale, outside Perth.

So the to-ing and fro-ing of the letters began. Patrick's family has told me that on the day he received the first letter from me, he ran down the main street of the village, waving the missive aloft and shouting over and over again to all and sundry:

"I've got a letter from Roy Hill" – only in French, of course!

So now, Patrick and Joseph had accomplished at least part of their overall plan, it only remained to account for the other three missing crew members. George and I were able to explain about our Navigator, Arthur Clarke and how, although being seen to bale out, nothing was ever seen of him subsequently. We had been flying east to west when shot down. Of the five that jumped, Bill and Eric landed on the German side of the Rhine, while George and I finished up on the French side. So we concluded that Artie, who was the third to jump, must have landed in the river, which was in full spate, following a prolonged period of incessant rain. Yet again the gods had smiled upon me – but for certain hiccups I would have made my exit at about the same time as Arthur.

So that left Bill and Eric to be accounted for. Neither George nor I had seen or heard from either of them since the War, so in order to try and locate them, we were going to have to 'do a Patrick.'

I remembered Eric had once told me he had been born in Kent and raised in Liverpool and that his dad had flown with the Royal Flying Corps in the First World War – that really was scant evidence on which to base a man-hunt!

After sundry inquiries had proved fruitless, I wrote to my elder brother Geoff, living in Durham, telling him of my quandary and asked if perhaps he had any thoughts on the subject. At the time London Weekend Television was running a programme called *Searchline Special,* fronted by Cilla Black and Geoff suggested it might be a good idea to enlist their help. Indeed he went one better and wrote to them himself, eloquently pleading my case.

The LWT people swung promptly into action and sent an attractive researcher named Joanna Stewart to interview me at home. It was arranged that I visit their studio near Tower Bridge in London, so that I could record an interview by camera, stating who I was trying to contact and why. In the event I made a terrible hash of the would-be interview, fluffing my lines and in general proving to be the opposite to photogenic. Undaunted, they said they would do whatever was possible to further my case, although as they were inundated with requests, it might be some time before they could find a slot for my 'find Eric' plea.

Eventually, about a month after brother Geoff's letter, I heard that, subject to pressures of time, my appeal was to be televised on Sunday 23rd April, 1989 at 10 p.m. Gill and I sat holding hands, eyes on goggle-box, scarcely daring to blink, lest we miss the vital item. When at last it came, it was somewhat of an anti-climax, just a picture of me, taken on my visit to Tower Bridge and the voice of a professional television 'type', giving a very brief synopsis of how I was involved in a Lancaster that crashed in Alsace in 1944 and if anyone knew the whereabouts of Eric Dunn, our Flight Engineer, would they phone LWT pronto. The whole shebang couldn't have lasted more than a minute.

There we sat, willing our phone to ring, but nothing happened. Then the following morning it did ring. I answered and a pleasant female voice said: "Is this Roy Hill?" I replied in the affirmative and the voice continued; "This is Jean Dunn, Eric's wife!" I honestly can't remember the subsequent conversation, my mind was in a whirl. I know that Jean told me that Eric was alive and well and would I like to talk to him? Of course, I couldn't see him, but after the gap of 45 years the voice sounded familiar and I instantly connected it with the tall slim wavy-haired 19 year old he had been when we'd both said goodbye to PB 765 in rather a hurry.

It was amazing how the time-gap seemed to be bridged in a trice; we had so much to say that it was hard to know where to begin, as our knowledge of one another's whereabouts and doings ceased abruptly on 4th December, 1944.

Eric's adventures after the crash made mine pale into insignificance. He was captured soon after landing by soldiers wearing field grey, but speaking a language that was anything but German – in fact they were Russians – White Russians, who had enlisted in the German Army to fight the Reds. After interrogation at Dulag Luft, where he seems to have had an easier ride than George, Bill and myself, he became one of many POWs who foot-slogged across Germany to Stalag Luft 7 right over near the Polish border. By the time they reached their destination, the Russians were advancing West across Poland, so the unfortunate Kriegies were obliged to back-track, walking hundreds more miles across the whole breadth of the Fatherland to the Dutch border, from where they were flown home at the cessation of hostilities.

Eric the modest, made light of "the big walk," as he referred to it, but one only has to glance at a map of Europe to realise what a feat of endurance it was, living off a war-ravaged land as they journeyed, in the face of great hostility, for month after month.

He finished up with feet in the most pitiable state and relates how on his return (like me he was taken to Cosford), he was presented with a superb pair of boots, with supple leather uppers. After trying them on, he went for a bath, leaving his clothes in the changing room. When he went to dress, the beautiful boots, his pride and joy, had gone missing!

After the War, Eric stayed on in the RAF for several years when he met and married Jean, was promoted to Warrant Officer and served on yet more Lancs and also Short Sunderlands, the splendid flying boats that did such sterling work with Coastal Command all through the war years.

After leaving the RAF he swapped uniforms and joined the Police Force, being stationed initially in Liverpool (where I had made many fruitless inquiries) and then being transferred to Dawlish, in Devon, only a few miles from where my own mother was born and bred. Here they settled, raised a family and when Eric eventually retired, they bought a house in the town.

So, thanks to *Searchline Special,* the gulf of years was bridged and now, of course, Eric was also in touch with George, so to Patrick and Joseph's unbound delight, three of the four known survivors had been contacted; it only remained to find the elusive Bill Wulff to complete the picture.

His only known address was in Wagga Wagga, New South Wales, but inquiries in that area drew a blank, so George, being a little more 'local' than Eric and I, volunteered to continue the campaign.

Early in the saga, when he had received the initial letter from Ron Winton, George had sent a copy of Ron's letter and one of his own, to Bill's old address, but to no avail. Eventually, George tracked Bill down to an address at Batemans Bay N.S.W. – he even got his phone number, but again a wall of silence.

Then, in April 1989 came the break through. George, phoning Bill's number yet again, was surprised, to say the least, when a man's voice answered the phone and within seconds the two old crew-mates were deep in conversation. It appears that Bill's wife had recently died and he had vacated his home and gone to live with friends. Now he had returned home to try and pick up the threads of a shattered life, and catch up with his mail!

Bill, now 73 years of age, was not enjoying the best of health, as I learned when, after a break of 44 years, I received a long, absorbing letter from him. It was hard to reconcile this descriptive epistle with the droll, laid-back character I had known as a young man, always so sparing with words.

So once again the letters flooded back and forth between England, Alsace and Australia. All at once, the long lost art (as far as we were concerned) of letter-writing was resurrected, as we tried to fill in all the blank pages, sending each other family photos and even some taken during the War. Among these was one of George, taken at the Stalag! He must be one of the very few who were POWs and have pictures to prove it!

*(l. to r.) Eric, Roy and George, taken at Paignton, 1990*

## CHAPTER FOURTEEN

# ALSACE ROLLS OUT THE RED CARPET FOR US

Patrick, whose English is limited, is fortunate in having a younger brother, Marc, who speaks our language far better than he writes it and a sister, Sabine, who is a brilliant linguist, working as a trilingual secretary (French, German, English) for a financial institution just over the Swiss border in Basel. So these two were instrumental in keeping all parties informed about the progress of the late PB 765, or rather, the survivors of that ill-fated plane.

Gradually, by correspondence and the exchange of photographs, we were introduced to numerous members and friends of our 'French family,' as we came to know them. Then a letter from Sabine told us that the village of Holtzwihr was planning a celebration at the end of June, 1989. It was hoped that George, Bill, Eric and myself would all be able to make the journey to Alsace and meet up with the folks of Holtzwihr, who, it seemed, symbolically linked our downfall in 1944 with the liberation of their village.

It was my great hope that all four of us would get together at 'the scene of the crime', but sadly it was not to be. Eric and Jean, who frequently holiday abroad, had already booked a stay in sunnier climes, while Bill's spirit was willing, but he was not physically up to the marathon trip half-way across the world. George, however, was keen as mustard and looked forward to showing Enid the land of the Poms.

It was arranged that they would come to England, do a sort of Cook's Tour, ending up at my home at Girton, near Newark, from whence we would wend our way by train across France, to meet up with all those involved in our very personal piece of 'Hitler's War.'

Excitement mounted as the great day drew nearer. Eric wrote to say that his son Kerry was about to marry his girlfriend Jill in May and that their honeymoon was to be spent touring the continent by motorbike. Kerry had inherited his love for this mode of transport from his Dad, being of a similar technical bent, although the latest BMW he rode was a far cry from Eric's old Triumph which was quite a veteran when together we explored the highways and byways of Lincolnshire.

On their return, the honeymooners painted such a rosy picture of Alsace and the warmth of their reception at Holtzwihr that we were wishing the time away, so that we could meet in the flesh these people for whom we already felt such a close kinship.

George and Enid had arranged to arrive in England on 20th June 1989, so their sight-seeing was going to be strictly limited, as the big day in Alsace was the 28th and the news from Patrick was that the village had raised money to pay for our accommodation from the evening of the 27th to 4th July and that, following a reception at the Mayor's parlour, a visit was to be made to the site of the crash, with the television cameras in attendance. It seemed inconceivable that, after half a life-time, this whole sequence of events had suddenly erupted, and we were being carried along by their momentum.

On 21st June our phone rang. I lifted the receiver and a voice said: "Is that Roy Hill?" There was no mistaking it; even though the accent was unmistakably Aussie, it could only be George. It really is extraordinary how, no matter what changes in appearance may manifest themselves, voices seem to have something timeless about them – this one certainly had! Straight away I visualised the handsome, wavy-haired pilot of yester-year, even though I knew, by dint of many photographs recently received, that the wavy hair no longer was and that time had left its indelible stamp on my old mate, as indeed it has on all of us.

After we had exchanged pleasantries, George handed the receiver to Enid and for the first time I heard the voice of the No.1 pin-up girl of Stalag Luft I – she sounded, as I knew she would, charming.

They had spent a few days in and around London and were going to visit friends in Northampton, who had kindly offered to bring them up to the wilds of Girton. They were scheduled to arrive at about 1 p.m. At a little after noon we realised that our supply of milk was rather deficient, so I drove the three miles to the nearest source of supply in the village of Collingham. On my return there was a strange car parked outside our property. I unlatched the garden gate and was half-way up the gravelled garden path when there was a shout from the house and there was George rushing to meet me, looking so different from 1945, but as extrovert and bouncy as ever. Following close behind came Enid, face wreathed in smiles. After embracing and back-slapping, we retired to the house to try and fill in the gaps left by all the years in between. As I suppose usually happens in these unusual circumstances, the conversation started with "do you remember?" – and just took off.

We proudly introduced our Aussie guests to our three children, all red-heads (as indeed I had been at their age). There was Kate, aged 29, a teacher by profession and a fitness fanatic whose very exuberance left one exhausted. Jenny, her junior by 21 months, came next; very like her sister in many ways, but slightly less volatile, she was (and is) an extremely talented self-employed artist and designer, with an impish sense of humour. I would love to think her expertise was inherited from me, but one look at my shovel-like hands puts the damper on that theory.

Last but not least, by any means, there was son Robin, baby of the family, being 23 at the time and at over 6 feet, dwarfing the rest of us. He had obtained a good degree (with honours) in Geography from Sheffield University and after searching around for inspiration, had finally plumped for a career in my old trade of photography (with absolutely no coercion from me). He and George struck up an immediate rapport, the age gap seemingly non-existent.

The following day we were to start the trek to Alsace, but a strike by British Rail thwarted our plans to reach Dover in time to link up with the train from Calais, which was to take us all the way to Colmar, where we were to be met. Robin volunteered to drive us all the way to the South Coast in the tiny Nissan Micra he had hired. Somehow, George, Enid, Gill and myself, in addition to the driver, wedged ourselves into the confined space, submerging ourselves under no less than seven items of luggage (they had 5 cases and we had 2). Not exactly an illustrious start to the great adventure! Luckily, we had telephoned ahead to some friends who live at Deal and who had agreed to put us up for the night, in order for us to catch the early morning ferry from Dover. So, as dawn was breaking, Robin duly delivered his out-size load to the Docks. I seem to remember a Lancaster being a bit cramped for room, but compared to that Nissan it was palatial.

The journey across Northern France was anything but inspiring, being an apparently unending succession of industrial sprawls and the unnatural contours of slag-heaps rearing their ugly heads rather like a moonscape without the romance. As we neared Alsace, however, the scenery changed dramatically as we entered countryside that the hand of man seemed to have enhanced rather than despoiled, with the terraced vineyards clinging to the hillsides, as they have done since Roman times and the picturesque villages that gave the appearance of having grown rather than being built.

At long last, having changed trains at Mulhouse with some delay, we arrived, rather travel-weary, in Colmar, at about 10 p.m., just as it was getting dark. Somewhat anxiously we peered around, looking hopefully to see a familiar face, when we were approached by a very large young man with a wide, welcoming grin – unmistakably Patrick. After effusive greetings, he led us into the station proper, where, under a lamp stood a little knot of about a dozen people, with faces abeam – our reception committee. What a delightful gesture! We had expected a car, or perhaps two, as we knew that Holtzwihr was about 5 kilometres from Colmar. But this was to be no back-door entrance and the feeling of goodwill generated by this group of Baumanns and friends was palpable.

I think it was at that moment that I became a confirmed Francophile. To people of my generation, the seemingly pathetic collapse of France in the face of the German onslaught of 1940 had left a lasting impression of indolence and apathy. Yet here we were being welcomed to the bosom of this little village that had been all but erased from the map by the horrors of war and by people with surnames like Baumann, Streicher, Meyer and Iwanski! These wonderful people of Alsace speak French, German and a patois all of their own, which appears to be a mixture of the two and reflects the chequered history of the region. Despite all those Germanic sounding names, however, a more patriotic assembly of Frenchmen would be hard to find.

After profuse greetings all round in typical Gallic fashion, we were bundled into cars and a little motorcade set off for the short journey to Holtzwihr. George, usually so voluble, was rather quiet, with a remote look in his eyes and I guessed that our thoughts were on a similar tack, thinking back to when we had last been in this locality, under entirely different circumstances.

Eventually we arrived at our destination, which proved to be a delightful guest-house in the village, run by Roger and Lillian Meyer. Here started the almost embarrassing hospitality that was extended to us during our stay in Alsace.

The following day we were introduced to numerous members of the Baumann clan, as well as many friends. There appeared to be, among the locals, a wonderful

*Gill and Roy with 3 canine companions in the kitchen, Girton*

*Woodpecker Cottage, Girton – our rural retreat*

*Roy and George with Patrick – doing our 'tele' interview*

*Our two gunners finally at rest, Choloy Cemetary*

*We three, Roy, Eric and George at 'the scene of the crime'*

*The finders and the found, with the largest artefact to survive
l. to r. Patrick, Joseph, Roy, Eric, George*

*Plaque donated by Eric's mum, Holtzwihr Churchyard*

*Gill and I laying a spray of English Poppies on an Alsatian War Memorial,
27th January 1995 – Lest We Forget*

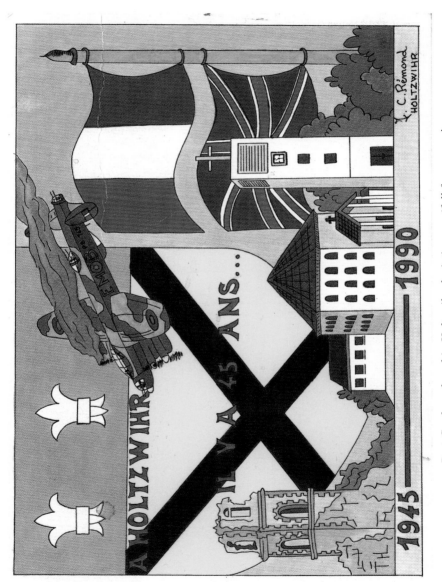

*Post Card produced in Holtzwihr depicting our 'fall from grace'*

*M'sieur Le Mayor with Lancaster model*

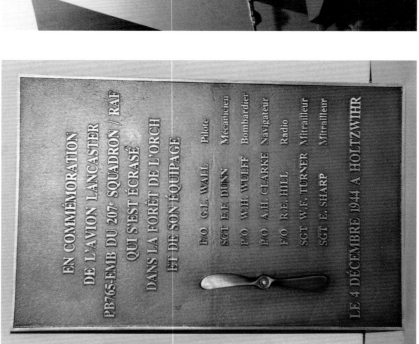

*Bronze plaque on the Village Hall, Holtzwihr*

spirit of comradeship, with humour bubbling just under the surface and occasionally bursting forth into gales of Gallic laughter. These people, despite terrible tribulations, had risen above it all; the hardships endured had created a bond that transcended all barriers of society, resulting in an atmosphere of 'togetherness' that we found delightfully contagious.

This was never more apparent than when Patrick took us to the home of his parents. He introduced them touchingly as Mummy and Daddy, a form of address that so suited them that we adopted them instantly. In fact is was some time later we discovered that their Christian names were Antoine and Annette.

'Daddy' was an extraordinarily fit 60 year old, who even at that advanced age, still occasionally turned out for the local soccer team! And I thought I was doing pretty well hanging up my boots at a mere 41! While Mummy, ever smiling, made us feel instantly at home, without a single word of English.

We were fortunate in having Patrick's sister Sabine to act as interpreter. There was so much we wanted to say and a 'go between' proved invaluable.

Patrick had converted a garage, beneath his house, into a museum, where were displayed many fragments of our old Lanc and a lump came into my throat at the sight of a boot sole. Was it Winky's or Ted's? Also an oxygen bottle – was it the one I grabbed before that frantic steeplechase down the fuselage and back up again, those many years ago?

The following morning, accompanied by many of the locals, and a television camera crew, we were escorted from the little village to the spot where 'B' Baker had finally come to earth. It was, for George and I especially, a very moving experience, one which we would rather have faced alone coming face to face with the past and reliving the traumatic events that had forever changed not only our lives, but numerous others. Perhaps, though, it was as well that we were supported by Gill and Enid while we surveyed the scene of the crash. The area is still densely wooded, but looking up, it was still possible to discern, where the trees were thinner, the direction the plane had taken in its death dive.

The television people bustled around, interviewing George and myself, asking the inevitable question – "How does it feel to be returning to the spot where your Lancaster crashed?" They had us pose, rather theatrically, clutching the only sizeable artifact visible at the site, a large chunk of rubber, presumably from one of the main-wheel tyres.

It was with some difficulty that I strove to prevent my mind dwelling on what at one time had been a recurrent nightmare – the sight of poor old Ted, limp and blood bespattered, hanging incongruously from his harness and Winky, huddled forlornly in what was left of his shattered turret, followed by that frenzied, seemingly endless, life-saving dash up the fuselage.

Perhaps it was as well that there were so many people around. After all, the British are not renowned for displays of emotion, and I mustn't let the side down!

Somehow we coped with the interview, wishing profoundly that Eric and Bill could have been there with us. Perhaps next time!

Returning to the village, we ended up at Patrick's house, to partake of a meal, laid on for friends and relations which, in typical Alsatian manner, went on, and on, and on. One has to learn, usually the hard way, to pace oneself on such occasions. I suppose that with Patrick being an employee of Pierre Sparr, owner of the local winery, it was natural that the famous wines of Alsace should be very much in evidence. There are, in fact, seven types of wine, six white and one rosé and I, hitherto no connoisseur, developed an immediate taste, especially for Reisling, with its bouquet and gorgeous fruity flavour. The locals, of course, being weaned on these extremely palatable concoctions were practically immune to them and empty glasses were replenished as if by magic.

Somehow we survived this gastronomic extravaganza, which was just as well, as on the following day we were to be guests of honour at an official reception at the Mairie, situated at the hub of Holtzwihr, a building that served as a village hall as well as a school.

Next morning, our hosts generously allowed us a little breathing space, to relax and recover from what had been a momentous day. The high emotions continued when, in the afternoon, we were ushered into the Mairie and into an upper room crammed with local notables, led by Pierre Fuchs, the Mayor. Speeches were made and toasts drunk to entente cordiale, to old comrades and new-found friends. All of which, while very impressive, left me rather floundering. After all, what had I done to justify being involved in all these festivities? By enormous good fortune I had managed to come through that fateful night in December 1944, when, let's face it, all that I'd done was to survive. There's nothing heroic in self-preservation!

But to our French friends we were symbols of their glorious liberation. when, in 1940, Alsace came under the jack-boot and all the young men, the flower of their youth, were conscripted into the Wermacht and, after a short period of training, were sent almost en bloc to the Russian Front. An enormous number (about 70%) never returned. Shortly after Holtzwihr had been liberated and the War in Europe ended, the tattered remnants of the 60,000 young Alsatians originally conscripted filtered slowly back to their homeland, only to find, as in Holtzwihr, their towns and villages laid waste.

Bearing all this in mind, I was better able to understand the workings of the French mind (even if the possessors of aforesaid minds had Germanic sounding names), after all, a little lionising never hurt anyone. So, fortified with these thoughts, I was able to shrug off my guilt complex and enter into the spirit of the celebrations.

That evening there was a dinner and dance at the village football ground, where yet again we were feted and introduced to numerous people; it really was wonderful to be wished well by so many – we were getting to like it!

After a further day of sight seeing and home visiting, it was time for us to return to England and normality, and revert to being a cog in a wheel, after a few heady days of being the wheel itself. George and Enid wanted to taste the flesh-pots of Paris, before returning to England for a few days, so Gill and I made our rather thoughtful way back to Calais. Our visit to Alsace had been a real eye-opener, with so much happening in so short a time.

We were soon jolted out of our reverie, however, when on arrival at Dover we discovered that the Rail Strike was still in operation and we were stranded. Luckily,

Gill espied a coach sporting Lincoln on its front, about to leave. A few words of supplication to the driver and we were aboard – crisis over!

Before leaving Holtzwihr, we had promised to return the following January (1990), when the 45th anniversary of 'la liberation' promised to be a momentous occasion and we were hoping all four surviving crew members would be able to attend.

*Self with just a bit of PB765*

# CHAPTER FIFTEEN

# MORE LIBERATION CELEBRATIONS

It was at the end of October that I received a letter bearing on its envelope the crest of Holtzwihr. (I wonder how many small English villages can boast one of those!). Gill and I were officially invited to attend the 45th anniversary celebrations of the liberation. The letter, signed by M'sieur le Mayor, spelled out in detail the programme of events for 27th January and most impressive it was. There would be the unveiling of a bronze plaque, erected on an exterior wall of the village hall, containing the names of the crew of PB 765, and all the relevant details of its demise; a presentation of medallions; a revue of Army and Air Force detachments (including a visit of the Royal Canadian Air Force), the opening of an exhibition organised by Patrick of W.W.II memorabilia (mostly bits and pieces of our old Lanc) and numerous model aircraft he had constructed over the years. Among those invited to attend were the British Ambassador to France, representatives of the French Government and, most important of all, the inhabitants of Holtzwihr. It was also hoped there would be a fly-past of military aircraft, and the icing on the cake was the very kind offer of free air passage to and from Basel, which, although in Switzerland, was the nearest airport to southern Alsace. We were also offered a week's accommodation in a Colmar hotel.

How on earth a small village of some 800 inhabitants could ever amass enough money to treat us in so regal a fashion (they did the same for Eric and Jean, not to mention George and Enid from Perth, W. Australia), I really have no idea. But one can imagine Patrick and his army of relations and friends beavering away at all manner of fund-raising activities.

My hopes that all four survivors would be present on the big occasion were dashed when George wrote to say he had at last met up with Bill Wulff. Enclosed with the letter was a photo of the two of them and it was evident that Bill was indeed a sick man; I could readily understand that travelling half-way around the globe would be a very taxing proposition for him, let alone having to face the rigours of the liberation festivities.

I received a long letter from Patrick, giving further details of additional preparations for the big event. It had been decided to erect some sort of monument in the woods, at the scene of the crash. He was hopeful of obtaining a Rolls Royce Merlin engine from one of the Lancs shot down on Guy Gibson's Dambusters Raid; it appears one had crashed not far from Holtzwihr, just across the Rhine, in Germany. The idea, I gather, was to re-build the engine to something like its former glory, then erect it, perpendicular fashion, on a plinth. This indeed would be a labour of love, involving an enormous amount of time and, I imagine, considerable expenditure.

Failing this rather ambitious plan, they were going to have a slab of locally quarried stone fashioned and suitably inscribed. I thought the latter suggestion to be a more practical proposition and so it ultimately transpired. There seemed to be no limits to the industry and resource of this Alsatian 'band of brothers', they were determined that future generations should be acquainted with the events that shaped the destiny of the world and their particular corner of it, in the mid 20th Century.

Gill and I were in frequent touch with Eric and Jean and they were very much looking forward to joining up with us for the short flight from Heathrow to Basel, which would be in stark contrast to the road/rail marathon of the previous June.

We were going to meet up with George and Enid at the hotel in Colmar. They were scheduled to touch down at Strasbourg, the capital of Alsace and were going to look around there before linking up with us.

It had been agreed that it would be an appropriate gesture to present to Holtzwihr some token as a souvenir of the great occasion and of our new-found friendship. After much heart-searching and exchange of letters, it was agreed that this should take the form of a brass model of a Lancaster. Eric and I were to obtain the actual model and George was going to get a plinth made from a handsome Australian hardwood called Jarrah, complete with two gold plated metal plaques, one stating the details of both the shooting down of PB 765 and the date the model was presented, and the other details of the crew and their various functions.

The plan was to marry the model and the plinth just before the ceremony, so there wasn't much room for error. When eventually we all three got together in a huddle at the hotel, the two fitted perfectly, except that the stem supporting the model was about an inch too long, a matter soon put to rights by a man with a hacksaw in the local hardware shop.

As on our previous visit, we were treated regally and the official parade, which took place in Holtzwihr village centre, was indeed an eye-opener. When we arrived, the locals were already out in force and there was a great air of expectancy. Everyone wore their Sunday best (even though it was Saturday) and some were attired in the picturesque national costume of Alsace.

The weather was reasonable for late January, dry, cloudy and chilly, which suited us, as that part of Europe can be distinctly inhospitable in winter (as I remembered all too well from 1944!). I know George and Enid were very relieved, coming straight from sunny Australia.

We six were directed to 'toe the line', alongside an array of military brass-hats and local and national dignitaries. I glanced at George, shoulders hunched against the cold, his face taut with emotion, then at Eric, who suffered from diabetes, also tense, with a faraway look in his eyes. I myself suffered somewhat from angina and it crossed my mind that, although we three were putting on a brave face, physically we were no match for our lady wives, who so resolutely supported us. Still, it was comforting to know that if one of us should keel over, help would be at hand!

We seemed to have stood for ages in our very conspicuous line, when suddenly the air was rent with the crash of cymbals and a rather discordant fanfare of trumpets and onto the square marched a bugle band of military cadets, followed by detachments of the French Army, more cadets and to give the occasion an authentic

Air Force flavour, an extremely smart squad of the RCAF.

Initially, as the first strident chords beat upon my eardrums, I had a sudden urge to laugh; it seemed to give the occasion an air of farce. But looking around at the multitude of solemn faces, I realised that to these wonderful people, who had suffered so grievously under the Nazi tyranny, this ceremony was a reminder of the years spent under the thrall of a despot. Later in the day there was to be a celebratory banquet, when their liberation would be joyously remembered, but this was also a time for sober reflection and thanksgiving.

The various marching groups were directed to pre-arranged locations on three sides of the little square. On the fourth side, which was kept clear, was the village hall, on one wall of which, draped in a French tricolour, was mounted the bronze plaque containing a potted history of us and our ill-fated Lanc. Above it were displayed on one side a large Union Jack and on the other another tricolour.

A microphone had been erected nearby and a hush descended on the gathering as speeches were made, by a government representative, a high-ranking army officer and by Pierre Fuchs, the Mayor. Before the latter began talking, we were handed an English translation of his speech, which had a very moving effect upon the assembly, us included. It ran as follows:

"45 years have passed since the liberation of Holtzwihr.

"Our village was not spared the ravages of war. 90% of it was destroyed and 33 people both civilians and military, were killed; their names are engraved on our War Memorial. The scars of many wounds and much suffering run deep, so that the memory does not fade.

"December 1944: the fight against Nazi Germany intensified. Almost every night Allied bombers flew across our skies in order to reach the enemy's targets. One of these aircraft was hit by German flak and crashed in the woods near Holtzwihr. Thanks to patient and thorough research by two of our community, Patrick Baumann and Joseph Barthelemy, today we are able to welcome three of the surviving crew of this aircraft: the British, Roy Hill and Eric Dunn as well as the Australian George Wall.

"On behalf of the people of Holtzwihr, of the village council and myself, I would like to honour them as well as their British friends, William Turner, Edward Sharp and A.H. Clarke, and specially thank them on the occasion of this anniversary ceremony.

"Our thoughts and gratitude also go to all those who fought and gave their lives to free our village and our country, France, so that peace and democracy live on. Current world events show to those nations who have paid the cost that these values are eternal."

Pierre Fuchs, Mayor of Holtzwihr

Then George, Eric and I were asked to step forward, facing the plaque, which the Mayor unveiled to the click of innumerable cameras. As we stood there, bare-headed, our thoughts went out to our less fortunate crew-mates who had been sacrificed to the gods of war, just three of Bomber Command's horrendous total of 55,000 lives lost – what a ghastly, mind sapping statistic.

That morning, just before the parade, Patrick and his brother Marc had approached us in some agitation. It had been discovered that the plaque, already in situ, had one very important defect – the Colmar firm who had produced it, had somehow managed to omit Arthur Clarke's name! There being insufficient time to rectify the error, it was decided to go through with the unveiling and swap it for a suitably amended version as soon as possible. We felt so sorry for our hosts, who had gone to great lengths to ensure that their (and our) great day should go without a hitch, but amazingly, no-one queried the fact that this Lancaster had a crew of only six and the change-over was accomplished shortly after our return to England.

Following the unveiling, there was a ceremonial laying of wreaths at the nearby War Memorial, where, among an impressive array of tributes, we placed small wooden crosses, each with a single poppy, in remembrance of Winky, Arthur and Ted. At the end of this moving ceremony, I had a great feeling of relief; after all the intervening years, our mates had finally been laid to rest, here among these friendly warm-hearted people of Alsace.

Finally, the various contingents marched from the village square to the stirring sound of the Marseillaise. Thus far, it had been a day to remember, but it was by no means over yet.

We were ushered into the village hall to find it bedecked with the flags of all nations and tables set to form a horse-shoe, sufficient to accommodate about 100 people. There ensued a meal that, interspersed as it was with speeches and presentations, ran from lunch to tea-time, in all about four hours! One lasting memory was of a table laden with all manner of sweet dishes. The ladies of the village seemed to have vied with one another as to who could produce the most mouth-watering concoction and the resulting dishes tasted just as good as they looked.

Naturally, being Alsace, the local wines were much in evidence and as the afternoon drew on, the occasion became more and more convivial. Half way through, the village priest, a cheerful, rather elderly chap who seemed to have a strong rapport with his flock (Holtzwihr was predominantly Catholic); disappeared for a few minutes, to return brandishing two unlabelled bottles of innocuous-looking liquid, which he proceeded to dispense to all and sundry. One taste was enough – the fiery hooch burned the throat and made the eyes water – and all this from a man of God! I know the Bible extols the virtues of a little wine being a good thing, but this was taking things to extremes! Amazingly, the faces around me beamed with pleasure as they supped the oh so potent brew – they were obviously hardy souls, with presumably fire-proof throats. It transpired that this 'fire-water' (their interpretation) was distilled from locally grown Mirabelle plums and was the nearest I have ever tasted to the equally transparent distillation that wracked our undernourished bodies at the Stalag, Christmas 1944.

Sandwiched between courses, following the inevitable speeches, was the presentation, by the Mayor, of medallions, to citizens of note and us, the guests of honour. They were cast in bronze, quite large (2 inches in diameter) and chunky; on the facing side was the Holtzwihr crest, surrounded by a laurel wreath, and bearing the legend "Commune de Holtzwihr" and on the reverse of mine it read "À Roy Hill. 45c Anniversaire de la Liberation 27 Janvier 1990." It is the only decoration I have ever received and it is very much treasured.

George, Eric and I in our turn presented our model Lancaster and it was received on behalf of the village by M. Fuchs. Then it was time for us to say a few words. George had a well rehearsed speech, in fact he seldom had to refer to his notes, and, as I knew he would, made a good job of it. As for me, I had been attending French language classes for a few months, in a belated effort to at least learn the basics; but I'm afraid that I found the language barrier just that – it almost amounted to a mental block. So I wrote out a short speech in English, got my teacher to tape it in French and in a last despairing effort, attempted to learn it phonetically. When it came to the crunch, however, my nerve deserted me after one paragraph and I shame-facedly reverted to my native tongue. Eric said a few brief words and our efforts were greeted with prolonged applause, some of which I suspect was engendered by the 'fire-water'.

Patrick and his team had gone to considerable trouble and expense to produce a 24 page souvenir brochure of the great day. The front cover, designed by a near neighbour of the Baumanns, depicted, in vivid colours, our Lanc, complete with the correct lettering and numbers, plummeting to earth, both starboard engines ablaze. It was set within a shield bearing the Holtzwihr coat of arms, with a picture of the shattered remains of the old church and one of the new one, together with the French tricolour and a Union Jack. The same design was repeated on a post-card and copies of both were on sale to the public, to help defray costs. We were asked to autograph copies and were only too pleased to oblige. For upwards of an hour we sat, industriously scribbling; thank goodness mine was a short signature!

At last this enormously enjoyable marathon began to lose momentum and someone suggested we pay a visit to the schoolhouse, where Patrick and his friends had mounted their display of Lancaster artifacts, all meticulously labelled and numerous models of war-planes of 'our' era, that had been constructed over several years.

The week before our arrival, the largest piece of 'B' Baker had come to light, being found in the barn of a nearby farm. It was a wing-tip section, about eight feet in length and was in exceptionally good condition. We three posed beside this tangible relic, feeling that we too were museum pieces, which I suppose we were and are. As the cameras flashed, Patrick and Joseph joined us, forming a little group of the finders and found.

It had been quite a day, but was not yet over. As the crowds dispersed, we retired to Patrick's home, there to watch the television 'rushes' on the Alsace news programme. Holtzwihr's great day to mark the breaking of the Teutonic chains had been well and truly televised and we were so proud to have had the privilege of sharing in the event and as we sat watching, I felt somewhat guilty; we seemed unwittingly to have lionised proceedings at the expense of our French friends. Shortly we would return to the ordinary, mundane world, but meanwhile we were enjoying our little ego trip.

In addition to the model Lancaster, we had brought with us a brass statuette, depicting a W.W.II airman in full flying kit, gazing soulfully upwards. This we presented to Patrick and his industrious team, as a permanent reminder of our momentous visit.

Then Maurice Fromm, a friend of Patrick and a prominent citizen, produced, like a rabbit out of a hat, a complete video of the day's proceedings, taken by himself and friends. We found it fascinating, seeing the sequence of events from several different angles. Sitting back, in that convivial atmosphere, relaxing with a glass of Reisling, it was difficult to relate the rather pale, tense faces on the screen with the rosy, glowing features that now surrounded me; it's amazing what a difference a warm fire and a good glass of wine can do and of course the release of tension.

The following morning we, along with almost the entire village population, attended a service of thanksgiving at the Church. This replacement for the more traditional one destroyed in January 1945, was a complete contrast to the accepted format, being hexagonal in shape, rather modern and unpretentious on the outside. Inside, however, it was quite a revelation, very light and airy, with seating all around, facing inwards towards a central dais, on which sat the choir and the priest (he of 'fire-water' notoriety!). The service, despite being conducted, of course, in French, with a good measure of Latin, was a most moving one. The acoustics were admirable, the choir sang like angels and our friendly priest, whose English was on a par with my French, nevertheless battled his way through a little speech of welcome. Afterwards I obtained a copy of it, so I am able to quote. It ran:

> "Dearest English and Australian Friends, I don't speak English, but I will do my best to make you understand me. M. Fuchs, Mayor of Holtzwihr, the local council and all the inhabitants have been very glad of your presence on the great occasion of the Liberation Day of their village, which is for us the forty-fifth Anniversary.

> "This morning, speaking for myself and in the name of the parochial community, I wish you a hearty welcome to our Church, where during this office we will pray for all militaries and civilian victims and more specially for those three members of your crew, these men who far away from their native land have given their lives for the freedom of our country.

> "We will pray for peace in the world, as well, for all Head States, to make them work with all their strength, for such a tragedy will never happen again. We will never forget what you have done, for the Liberation of Holtzwihr.

> "Please accept our best wishes, as we send them to your families. Thank you very much."

It wasn't so much the words, but the sheer sincerity of the man that so impressed us; never have I come away from a service with such an inner glow. I was thinking of that other priest, the one that had lain Winky and Ted to rest, all by himself; it would be nice to think that he was of the same calibre.

Following the service, we were taken to see the spot in the little graveyard where our two mates had lain for a few years prior to being removed to a military cemetery.

We rather regretted that they had been moved – the place had such an air of tranquility about it.

Then we went once more to 'the scene of the crime', I was forgetting that Eric and Jean had never been there. The forest was cold and forbidding, unlike the previous June, when all was sunlight and leafy shade. We saw for the first time the stone that our friends had erected at the site. It was a simple oblong block of locally quarried stone, about three feet high and two wide and was a pleasing mixture of grey and pink. On the front it bore the inscription "ICI EST TOMBE AU COMBAT LE LANCASTER PB 765 DE LA ROYAL AIR FORCE 4.XII.1944." Many photos were taken both of us and our Alsatian friends, in fact a little later we were deluged with pictures taken by so many people and as a consequence we have a wonderful pictorial record.

*At the Crash Scene*

This visit concluded the week-end's 'official' functions and the next three days were a delightful holiday. We were taken to see many of the surrounding towns and villages, the pick of which was Riquewihr, a walled medieval town, which had magically escaped damage by war and was a beautifully preserved time capsule. We also had time to explore Colmar, that most gracious of towns and Joseph took us to see his place of work, in the ancient local library and we watched fascinated as he demonstrated the time-honoured skill of bookbinding, using equipment that had been unchanged for centuries.

We were wined and dined firstly at the home of the Mayor, such a pillar of Holtzwihr society. He asked if we hoped to be available again in 1995, when the 50th Anniversary celebrations would be held. I said we would be honoured to attend, God willing, but would he still be Mayor? Yes, he said, as elections were only held every seven years for that office and he had only been incumbent for a year.

The following evening we were invited to the home of Mr. and Mrs. Maurice Fromm, M. Fuchs's right hand man. At the end of yet another marathon, beautifully prepared meal, he presented each of us with a souvenir copy of the video we had already seen. His hobby was running (and participating in) a group of Alsatian folk dancers, who are really a sight to behold in their gorgeous national costumes. They tour all over the world, waving the flag of Alsace everywhere they go and, I've no doubt, enchanting everyone with their infectious spirit of bonhomie.

One other visit of note was Mulhouse, to the National Automobile Museum, advertised as "The World's Most Marvellous Motor Museum" and having been there, I wouldn't dispute the claim. There were over 500 beautifully preserved cars of all nationalities, but pride of place goes to the worlds largest collection of Bugatti's (112 in all). These cars were collected by the brothers Schlumpf, who went bankrupt in 1976 and the collection became the property of the Museum.

We were scheduled to fly from Basel on Wednesday afternoon and on Tuesday evening our ever attentive hosts took us to a delightful restaurant, where the fare exceeded all the preceding gastronomic delights. Unfortunately, my stomach rebelled, and I had the miserable experience of watching everyone else tucking in to a gourmets feast, the very sight of which repelled me. Gill had been bitten by the same bug when we arrived, but had soon recovered, so I was hopeful of a quick recovery, but at that moment it was scant comfort.

I looked around the table; most of those present had been in the group at the station on our arrival. Patrick, of course, was very much in evidence, although his wife Rolande was unable to attend, having to stay at home and look after their two children, Carine and Valerie. Daddy and Mummy sat opposite us, radiating good-will. We were, of course, unable to converse, but Sabine made a speech on her Mum and Dad's behalf, eloquently voicing some of their sentiments, which brought a lump to the throat. Next to Sabine sat her husband Julian, quiet and thoughtful, son of a Polish airman who sought haven in England when Hitler invaded his homeland in 1939. Next to Joseph sat his nephew, Bruno, yet another quiet, likeable young man, an industrious unsung worker in 'the cause'. Then there was Antoine (Tony) and Martine, his wife, great friends of the Baumann family, cheerfully supportive of Patrick and his endeavours, sitting next to Marc and his fiancée Danielle, soon to be his wife. Maurice Fromm and his wife were also in evidence, chatting away about the next trip of the Alsace dancers, which I understood was to be Thailand. Others there most certainly were and but for my indisposition they would probably come to mind.

And so this, the best meal I never had, came, like all good things, to a close. It only remained for us to make a protracted series of goodbyes, as we were going straight from the hotel to Basel the following day. George and Enid were going to make their way to Frankfurt, there to catch a plane for Aussie. I warned George, should he be anywhere near the railway station there, to keep an eye open for flying missiles, but that I understood the natives are a little more friendly these days!

The following day, laden with good wishes and mementos, we were whisked to the airport. It had been an unforgettable week, packed with incident and nostalgia – something for the grand-children to tell their grand-children.

Poor old Eric discovered, on the plane, that his treasured medallion had gone missing and despite feverish searching, it never came to light. It was subsequently replaced by an understanding and compassionate Holtzwihr, but someone, somewhere, possesses a large, attractive medallion with the name Eric Dunn engraved on it – hope it brings him (or her) bad luck.

Upon our return we received, by post, another video, taken by the television cameras covering the events of 27th January, all done in a most competent and professional way. Showing it saves an awful lot of verbal explanations and is far more graphic.

Eric rang shortly after, saying that when we visited the churchyard in Holtzwihr, he thought it a good idea to erect an inscribed tablet where our two gunners had originally been laid to rest. In due course, this was done, the cost being generously defrayed by Eric's mother. The tablet, of attractive dark marble, bears the RAF crest and the wording reads: "In memory of three comrades who flew in Lancaster PB 765 207 Sqdn Spilsby died in action 4 December 1944."

So now there are no less than three tangible memorials in or near the village. Patrick wrote to say that a sign-post had been erected in the forest, pointing towards 'B' Baker's last resting place and that it is a favourite walk for the villagers on a sunny Sunday afternoon.

Gill thought it would be a nice gesture if we sent some bulbs and plants from England, to transport a little of the English countryside to our own spot in an Alsatian wood. So Marc and Danielle, who sometimes come to England, returned home with a few examples. We are hoping, on our next visit, to see a few English primroses peeping through the undergrowth, or maybe some violets, daffodils or crocus. There is one possible snag, apart from the difference in climate; wild boar still roam the forests of Alsace and they are notorious herbivores!

So our adventure, which suddenly mushroomed after over 40 years, as a result of the curiosity and tenacity of two young men, came, or almost came, to an end. But as the song says – "The melody lingers on," and things will never be quite the same again; as I said to Patrick when we parted – "See you in '95!"

# CHAPTER SIXTEEN

# OUR CONTRIBUTION TO EUROPEAN UNION

S ince penning what I thought were the final words of *Survivor,* a few very important facts have come to light.

Since those heady days in January 1990, both Patrick and his brother Marc have been beavering away at their hobby-horse – unearthing every possible detail concerning the aircraft of all nationalities that came to grief in their area of Alsace during hostilities. Their researches brought some surprising results, which altered some long-standing theories.

We, who survived, had always believed we had been the victims of predicted flak, at which the Germans were so proficient. Our only recollections of those last horrendous moments were of sudden explosions, followed by fire and mayhem – from then on we were automatons, reacting to the many hours of 'bale-out' drill previously rehearsed, allied to a primeval instinct of self preservation.

Imagine my surprise then, when, in December 1990, I received a letter from Marc telling me that, as a result of extensive inquiries, it had been established that we were in fact shot down by a German night-fighter! The evidence they had amassed was astonishing. Our executioner, it appears, was one Karl Friedrich Müller, commander at that time of the 1$^s$ night-fighter group based at Darmstadt. They flew Me109s equipped with the then German secret weapon, upward firing cannon, known as 'Schräge Musik' which wrought such havoc on Bomber Command during the latter part of the War. Karl was the top-scoring night-fighter pilot of the Luftwaffe, that is for single-engined aircraft, and according to the records, we were the 27th of his eventual tally of 30 victories. (Marc Baumann informed me that Müller had succeeded in installing upward firing cannon, normally fitted to 2-seater fighters, such as the Me110, 210 and 410, into his Me109G. Apparently his was a unique installation in a single-engined fighter). An entry in his Log Book, giving the exact location and time of our demise (with typical German thoroughness), put the matter beyond doubt. We were one of his two victims that night, both of which were shot down within a few minutes of each other and both were Lancasters.

Unfortunately, Karl Müller died in 1987, precluding any sort of re-union. It would have been nice to have heard his side of the story.

So these revelations finally set the seal on the PB 765 saga, effectively tying up all loose ends, but not for those intimately concerned with the escalation of events. The friendships established would endure; I know our lives have been enriched by being in contact with our 'French family' and I'm sure the younger generations will keep up the good work.

SURVIVOR

Christmas 1992 brought with it the usual flood of greetings from our friendly Alsatians. Among them was one from Marc, enclosing a head and shoulders photo of Karl Müller, resplendent in a uniform adorned with the Iron Cross. In the background is part of his Messerschmitt with many RAF roundels, complete with dates and clearly visible are two bearing the legend 4.12.44 – which one was us?

I showed the photo to Gill, who remarked – "Isn't he like Prince Charles!"

The years following the celebrations of 1990 passed with great rapidity. The letters flowed between the various players on the PB 765 stage, there were also several journeys made of varying length.

Patrick and his family honoured Girton with their presence. He asked if I would take him to Spilsby, a journey I hadn't made since 1945. He said that he'd seen where we landed and to see from where we took off would complete the picture.

So we made the pilgrimage. Spilsby aerodrome no longer exists; the site, like countless other airfields, has reverted back to its former rural self. However, there is still one hangar left standing, used presumably for grain storage, so it was possible to work out approximately where the various offices had been and bits of the old main runway still exist. Patrick was thrilled and his boundless enthusiasm was contagious, so that I almost forgot the sombre connotations that the place had for me.

Other visitors were Patrick's sister Sabine and her husband Julian, who brought Mummy and Daddy with them – the latters' first trip to England. Being country folk, they seemed to develop an immediate affinity with little Girton, which, with only 18 houses, is small even by Holtzwihr standards. I think the little cluster of mainly Georgian cottages reminded them of their village before its virtual destruction in January 1945.

On another occasion Patrick's brother Marc and Danielle, now his wife, spent a few days with us, taking back to France numerous bits of flora from the Woodpecker garden. Danielle immediately fell in love with our Golden Retrievers, and was reluctant to return home without at least one of them!

Naturally, when the various parties arrived, we wanted to show them as much of our local scene as time would permit and we got quite used to taking them on our local Cooks Tour, which usually included visits to the fabulous Lincoln Cathedral, the 'Cathedral in a village' at Southwell, the medieval market place in Newark and, a little further afield, the greatest of all stately homes, Chatsworth House, in Derbyshire. On these jaunts, we began to see England and its way of life through a visitor's eyes and the more we did it, the more patriotic we became.

Patrick wrote to tell me that a party of six was going to pay a visit to Australia. This consisted of Marc and Danielle, Joseph and his nephew Bruno and friends Tony and Martine. The holiday was to last about six weeks, culminating in an invasion of George and Enid's home in Attadale, near Perth. From all accounts, the visit was a memorable one – another by-product of Patrick's now historic 'plane in the forest' discovery.

The time drew near for the all-important 50th Anniversary of Holtzwihr's Liberation and we were thrilled at the prospect of renewing old acquaintances. The official invitation was rather late in arriving – it appears that the old Mayor had been replaced by a new one, causing some delay in the arrangements.

110

I contacted George and Eric and was dismayed when they both said, for one reason or another, that they would be unable to attend. So Gill and I decided we would have to be responsible for waving the flag on behalf of the crew.

As the events of 1990 had been televised by the French, we thought it a good idea to try and drum up some interest by British television and I approached the ITV Central people, based at Nottingham. At first their interest seemed rather luke-warm, but shortly before we left home to go to Heathrow, from where we were flying to Basel, they rang to say they were sending a reporter and a cameraman.

We had arranged for a weeks stay with Mummy and Daddy. There were to be several celebrations in southern Alsace, as many villages and towns had been liberated within the space of a few days. It appears we were to attend the Holtzwihr festivities and also a much larger event at Marcolsheim, on the banks of the Rhine, where, in 1944, I had spent those few horrendous days which caused me to have nightmares (in fact, still do!).

Our short flight was, to say the least, hectic. We arrived over Basel in a storm of great ferocity, the aircraft pitching in the most alarming manner before touching down – ours was the last flight that day, all others being diverted elsewhere.

Marc and Danielle were there to meet and greet us and as we left the terminus we could see the aftermath of the freak storm – dustbins and debris covered the road – what a reception!

Our welcome to Holtzwihr, though muted by comparison with previous ones, was nevertheless very warm, and during the next few days we were going to re-acquaint ourselves with the numerous members and friends of the Baumann clan, what a prolific and sincere bunch of people they are.

The day after our arrival we were visited by the television team from England. Central Television had sent one of their top and certainly most attractive, reporters in the shape of Sally Bowman and a charming young man to do the photography. They were esconsed in a hotel in Colmar and were to remain with us for the whole week. They took an enormous amount of footage, which on their return was reduced to an episode lasting just seven minutes! Sally was most helpful and I told her of the awful hash I had made of my only other attempt at being televised. This time I had a little more success, in fact I was almost coherent!

The official functions followed a similar pattern to the previous ones, except that the added significance of the 50 year period seemed to give the occasion an even more dramatic aura.

At the dinner following the parade at Holtzwihr, I was expected to say a few words – but this time I didn't attempt to speak in French. Instead, on going to bed the night before the function, on the back of an old envelope I wrote:

"Ladies and Gentlemen of France. Five years ago, two of my fellow survivors and I, along with our wives, had the honour of being invited to share in your 45th liberation ceremony. The occasion was deeply moving for us all, particularly when you all joined us in remembering with gratitude the enormous sacrifices made by so many of our, and your countrymen. As a result, we have been able to enjoy living our lives to the full these 50 years. Let us never forget the debt we owe, that can never be repaid. We feel that our three friends who, in December of 1944 were sacrificed to the gods of war and are now laid to rest here in France, did not die in vain.

"We, who survived, are eternally grateful to our Alsatian friends, for their hospitality and the friendship so generously given.

"So from much pain and anguish has emerged this bond of friendship. Since we were last here in 1990, wonderful things have happened – the Berlin wall, so long a symbol of division, is now no more and the natives of Europe are finding that their common values far out-weigh their differences. Let us hope that mankind has at last learnt its bitter lesson, that to survive it has to co-exist, breaking down the barriers of language and culture.

"So here's to the future and may God bless our endeavours. VIVE LA FRANCE!"

The format for the occasion was very similar to that of 1990, except that I had no mates to bolster my confidence, or to hide behind! Gill, however, came to my rescue, giving a boost to my flagging morale when required. We were getting to enjoy our mini celebrity status – Girton was going to appear even quieter on our return, when our only audience would be a canine one!

The much larger celebration, held at Marcolsheim, was a real eye-opener. It was attended by thousands of inhabitants from the nearby villages and a large number of local and national dignitaries. There was a procession through the streets and in addition to the bands and contingents of Alsatian militia, there was a motorcade of W.W.II American military vehicles, with the personnel resplendent in GI uniforms, distributing largesse, in the shape of chewing gum and candies to the children as they chugged along at walking pace – just as the original liberators had done in 1945.

There was, of course, the inevitable banquet and this was held at a quite magnificent restaurant. Once again, the speeches were made and my offering, again written in bed the previous night (I was trying desperately to avoid repeating the Holtzwihr one – there were many who attended both functions) ran as follows:

"Citizens of France, 50 years ago I was here in Marcolsheim in very different circumstances. Having parachuted from a crippled Lancaster, I was taken prisoner by the Wehrmacht. It was three weeks before Christmas 1944, just before the terrible battles that laid waste so many beautiful towns and villages in Alsace, with such horrendous loss of life and human suffering.

"We remember with gratitude the enormous sacrifices made by so many of my, and your countrymen. As a result, we have been able to enjoy living our lives to the full these 50 years, a freedom bought with their blood. It is a debt we can never repay. We must make sure that all the pain and anguish were not made in vain and must cherish the liberty that we have inherited through them.

"So may peace, the greatest of all blessings, be upon us all. VIVE LA FRANCE."

At the banquet I was seated next to a venerable gentleman who, it transpired, was the local M.P., or its equivalent. His English was excellent (thank goodness) and in conversation I related to him the trauma of my previous sojourn in Marcolsheim and how I had witnessed the bombing and demolition of the large iron bridge across the

Rhine. I told him I had searched with no success for the place of my incarceration and was astounded when he said – "I know where you were, it was the old Customs House; if you wish I'll take you there."

So after the usual prolonged feast, he took Gill and myself on the short drive down to the river, where, perched on the bank, was the derelict, forlorn-looking Customs House. One glance was enough – there, facing the river and virtually at ground level, were two small windows – we had been in the basement! I turned to Gill and said – "I'm sure this is it – I'll know for certain when I see the courtyard." I needed no further confirmation. One look at the place and that same feeling of terror, first felt 50 years before, seemed to envelope and choke me – we beat a hasty retreat.

It appears that after the War, the bridge had been re-built about 100 metres downstream, rendering the Customs House redundant. I thanked our friendly guide and he was very understanding when I explained the reason I had been in such a hurry to vacate the area. He was a chap somewhere in his 60s and said he had heard rumours of the infamous goings on during the war at the Customs House and my version of events confirmed them. I only wish the television team had been there – it was the only time they were missing.

The Customs House revelation seemed to finalise things for me. It was as if, after 50 years, all the loose ends seemed to have been tied – it was the end of a saga.

Thanks to Patrick and his team, memories that had lain dormant for so many years had been resurrected and given life a new impetus.

Meeting and getting to know these sons and daughters of Alsace has been such an uplifting and rewarding experience. The links of friendship that have been forged will, I am sure, continue on into the future – our two family's contribution to European Union.

On our return to England, we watched on television our momentous week condensed into seven minutes – fame at last!

So it's back to anonymity, a world dominated by dogs and delphiniums, puppies and pansies.

Last year I marched past The Cenotaph on Armistice Day, one of a contingent of ex-POWs. As I stood on Horse Guards Parade just prior to moving off, I thought we looked rather a sorry bunch of oldies, but when the band struck up the RAF March Past (it was my first parade for 50 years!) heads were suddenly held high, backs were straightened and there was a spring in the step that belied our years. I felt an inner glow-once again. I was walking with the Gods – this race of super-men were still something very special. Marshal Vorishilov would, I am sure, have approved!

Dear Roy and Gil

Thank you for your postcard from your fantastic trip to the sun (New zeland, Thaiti ..). We were happy to here about you ; you seem to be in a good health, the marvelous trip must have improved it.

— The mayor of HOLTZWIHR and the council try to improve the memorial for the lancaster as they are able. So last year they baptized a new street « rue du Lancaster ».
The inhabitants don't all know what the Lancaster is but the old persons of HOLTZWIHR and the one who worked on the plan of the memorial are really proud of it.
During the spring a foothpass has opened in the forest. It pass over the memorial of the Lancaster in the forest and over another memorial for the US soldiers who liberated HOLTZWIHR.
Patrick was of course in the « team » who created this.

We are looking forward to there about you.

Yours faithfully        _Patrick, Rolande, Louise, Valérie_

family BAUMANN

*Latest News from Holtzwihr*

*Major Müller and part of his Messerschmidt*